HARDWIRED

FOR

LIFE

Human Understanding
Beyond
Surface Personality

BRAD KULLMAN

Discernment Press

Hardwired for Life

Copyright © 2017 by Brad Kullman

Published by Discernment Press
Powell, Ohio

Publisher's Cataloging-in-Publication data

Names: Kullman, Brad, author.
Title: Hardwired for life : human understanding beyond surface personality / Brad Kullman.
Description: Includes bibliographical references. | Powell, OH: Discernment Press, 2017.
Identifiers: ISBN 978-1-946324-00-9 | LCCN 2016918250
Subjects: LCSH Personality. | Human behavior. | Individual differences. | Brain--Popular works. | BISAC SELF-HELP / Personal Growth / General | PSYCHOLOGY / Personality
Classification: LCC BF698 .K85 2017 | DDC 155.2--dc23

Cover design and internal images by Bill Naughton

Printed in the United States of America

First Edition 2017

For further information on the topics in this book and the author, please see HardwiredLife.com and BradKullman.com

To Pam, my amazing wife and best friend. Thank you for being a constant reminder that true beauty extends far beneath that which is revealed on the surface.

Also, to A.J., Sophie, and Audrey, my three awesome children. Thank you for demonstrating every day how talent and giftedness manifests itself in so many forms.

And, finally, to my wonderful parents, David and Karen. Thank you for always believing in me and for your continuous encouragement to be the best me I can be.

Contents

Preface

The term "wired" is often used to characterize a person who is highly energized by an excessive amount of stimulants (caffeine, sugar, etc.). It is also used at times to explain the seemingly inherent cause of certain behaviors or personality traits, though normally without any substantive explanation as to why such a correlation might be so.

This book is the culmination of more than a decade of study and research aimed at not only comprehending, but also explaining a discovery that quantifies the root of human behavior, personality, and even performance. As I worked through this material, streamlining it for optimal ease of understanding, it became apparent that the best way to describe what is being observed is that we are not simply wired, but we are *"hardwired."*

While standard "wiring" can normally be reworked, or re-routed in some fashion, *hardwiring* is a preset structure that is not only integral to the operation of a device, but is inherently unchanging. Such is the case with what you will learn in this book. I often point out the similarity to handedness. We are each innately hardwired to be predominantly right or left-handed when it comes to specific tasks. Though we may be able to consciously use our other hand to some measure of effectiveness when making it a point to do so, we naturally return to using our more comfortable dominant hand when our focus changes. We don't know why this hand-dominance is so. We only know that it is an innate tendency that appears to be genetically hardwired in us at conception.

In this book, I explain in detail the various specific ways in which we are each predisposed toward certain thought processes and behaviors, supported by modern day advances in the hard sciences. As you will see, the correlations observed between motor skills and brain function lends strong evidence to a similar hardwired circuitry that drives a specific manner of thought, behavior and performance in every person.

While others may attempt to explain this discovery in some manner, I am confident that the method and terminology revealed herein is the most straightforward and comprehensible form available anywhere. Learning this revolutionary method of human understanding will forever change the way you look at yourself and those around you.

BRAD KULLMAN

Introduction

What if you could read other people's minds? Not their specific thoughts in the moment—that is only the fictional stuff of movies, of course—but rather to understand how their minds work. What if you could comprehend—and quantify—how they absorb and then process information from you, from others, and from the world around them?

What sort of difference could that knowledge make in your life? Think about it. As a parent, it could open a whole new world for relating to and guiding your children. You would instantly become more effective at disciplining, motivating, and directing your children into areas of interest in which they could excel. How many frustrations of parenting could such insight relieve?

In education, parents, as well as teachers, could have a tangible understanding of how to best motivate each student and how to relate subject matter, accordingly. In addition, subject areas in which each student might struggle could be identified and anticipated in advance. How might that transform the education process?

In relationships, it could provide a tremendous advantage in courting the object of your desires. It could help to make you a more appreciative and understanding spouse, thereby fostering a more loving family atmosphere. Think of past problems in your most important relationships. How many of them could have been remedied, or even prevented, if you better understood what—and why—the other was thinking?

In the world of sports, an athlete's mental toughness and intestinal fortitude is defined by the term, "makeup." The ability to quantify makeup has long been the "holy grail" of evaluators. In fact, the qualities that contribute to good makeup on the field of play are often quite different from those which support good makeup off the field. If you could effectively understand and quantify the way each athlete's mind functions, could you gain a more enlightened perspective in regard to both the athlete's performance and behavior? If you compete in sports yourself, even if only for casual recreation, how could you benefit from the ability to objectively comprehend and quantify the specific way in which your mind functions? This insight would enable you to implement optimal strategies designed specifically for you in order to perform at your mental peak!

Consider the workplace, which is often another, if more subtle, arena of competition. What if you could readily discern the manner in which each prospective customer would process information and custom tailor your sales pitch, accordingly? What if you could better understand how the mind of your boss works? Would it not make meeting expectations an easier proposition? Even internal office politics could be positively impacted if you could identify the inspirations and motivations of your coworkers. If you are the boss, how could this insight enable you to better manage and lead your subordinates?

Think about all of the people in your life, from the most important to a casual acquaintance. What if you possessed the ability to quickly ascertain how those around you would be naturally inclined to absorb and process what you say and do—before you say or do it? What if you could objectively predict how the people in your life would be apt to behave and perform in various situations and circumstances? Could that make a significant difference in your life? Perhaps most importantly, what if you could better understand why you feel, behave, and perform as you do?

The information contained in this book reveals a revolutionary method for understanding how each person thinks, why they behave as they do, and even why they perform the way they do—from the boardroom to the ball field. While previous attempts at human understanding share rather dubious origins, from psychiatric wards to the dictionary, this revolutionary breakthrough is based on the study of normal people doing ordinary things in everyday life.

This approach to understanding people is the first methodology to quantify psychological findings with the latest advances in neuroscience. It is predictably complex, yet remarkably simple. Just as the intricate human body has incredible complexity, and every person is unique, we can all be grouped together by some simple defining traits. For instance, every person is born with two arms and two legs, ten fingers and ten toes. Yet we can also be easily placed into subgroups, as well. Males and females are easily differentiated, of course, and can be placed into respective groups. We could also derive subgroups by hair color, eye color, height, weight, etc. The classifications you will learn with this technique are more intricate, yet simple to ascertain and quantify with patience and proper study.

Impressions First

We all meet new people, virtually every day, oftentimes without even realizing it. Sometimes it might be a formal introduction, such as at a meeting or social event. More often it is an informal setting, such as shopping in a store. Perhaps it is a store employee assisting us or ringing up our sale, or it could possibly be a fellow shopper. It may even be a passing stranger as we stroll along the sidewalk.

What is the first thing we do when we see/meet/interact with someone for the first time? Think about it. From the casual to the more formal setting, we immediately begin "sizing up" this new person. It may be hair, clothes, a smile, a scowl, a laugh, or something else that immediately has us categorizing our new acquaintance, even if only subconsciously. The categories may be as vague and simple as "nice guy" or "knucklehead." Frequently, we find ourselves gleaning more specific information. We may quickly pick up on clues that a person is outgoing or reserved, friendly or more impersonal, pragmatic or visionary, and even strict/rigid or more go-with-the-flow. Consciously or otherwise, we make evaluations of others all the time. We then incorporate these appraisals into the ways we communicate and otherwise relate to that person.

Everyone has heard the adage you only get one chance to make a first impression. We may think of this when we focus on a formal meeting with someone we consider to be "important," but the fact is we all make and evaluate first impressions virtually every day. While at one time it was considered that a first impression occurred within sixty seconds of meeting someone, subsequent research trimmed the estimated time to less than seven seconds. More recent findings reveal that the first—and often unchanging—impression of a stranger is made by seeing their face for one tenth of a second! How can this be so? A clue to this remarkable phenomenon, as well as many other answers to questions relating to human understanding, are revealed and discussed on the following pages.

The "Personality" Hunt

Human behavior and personality have been popular targets of theorists for quite some time. This quest to formally comprehend the thoughts and actions of people dates back to the ancient Greeks and ancient Egypt. Since at least that time, many have endeavored to explain the actions of mankind. The scientific discipline of psychology developed in the 1870s. More than simply the study of the psyche or mind, however, psychology is the investigation of human behavior, albeit from a limited perspective.

While the general public may have little use for the complexities of scientific psychology, most of us have questions about personality. Especially in recent years, personality tests seem to be everywhere. From job applications to marriage counseling to our favorite magazines, everywhere we turn somebody is urging us to learn what "color" or "season" or "animal" we are. But what are these "tests" really measuring?

"Personality" can be defined as the *sum total of the physical, mental, emotional, and social characteristics of an individual*. While we like to think that we are each unique—and we certainly are in some respects, there are definite observable patterns of behavior among people. For instance, we might easily categorize people as outgoing or reserved, meticulous or haphazard, etc. As we look carefully at an individual, we find that what appears to be random behavior may, in fact, be quite orderly and predictable. In fact, marketing research firms continue to quantify and group our behaviors with increasing success.

Commercial ventures into personality and human understanding date back to at least the early 1800s when "phrenology" involved feeling the rugged topography of a person's head in order to gather what supposedly lay within. As laughable as this practice in human understanding may be in retrospect, the idea that thoughts, emotions, character, and other behavioral traits are located in specific parts of the brain appears to be much closer to the mark than some other efforts to understand ourselves.

Today's favored mode of self-understanding comes in the form of commercial personality questionnaires. A handful of early efforts evolved into a multitude of forms that remain widely used today. In fact, commercial personality testing has become a 500-million dollar industry with over 2,500 different tests being taken by tens of millions of people every year.

Crazy Ancestors

Unfortunately, while well-intended, these efforts are woefully lacking in actionable substance. Very few users of today's "personality" mechanisms are aware of whence their origins may be traced. Even as advances in the hard sciences (neuroscience, genetics, biomechanics, optics) have revealed many commercial personality tests in use today to be invalid and unreliable, the market for them continues to grow, seemingly unabated. The thirst for self-understanding and self-help is just so great, as is the desire to better understand—and label—others.

Predecessors of today's tests have a strikingly common theme. Many present-day tests have evolved from versions that were originally constructed for use by mental institutions—derived from efforts to determine who was "crazy" and who was not. Even those not designed for categorization to that degree were often used to separate the "deviant" from the "normal." Today's versions are used to evaluate people in schools, the workplace, government, and even in our churches. Counseling of all forms often begins with some method of personality measurement. Other tests show up in the form of the "self-help" variety that enables people to fit themselves neatly into whichever personality description they unwittingly *desire*.

Look Closer

But what if everything you thought you knew about understanding and communicating with people was wrong? What if even the way you view yourself has been skewed for as long as you can remember? Though we may (desire to) see ourselves in a certain manner, others may often view us differently. There are many reasons for that, and neither perspective is correct one hundred percent of the time. Because we have a tendency to confuse nurture with nature, the picture of what makes each person the way they are is often difficult to clearly discern.

Ordinary People Doing Ordinary Things

While most of these endeavors to research "personality" over the years involved the study of the behavior of "abnormal" people (those suffering from schizophrenia, depression, and other mental illnesses), one researcher stands out. Swiss psychiatrist and psychologist, Dr. Carl Gustav Jung's discerning personality evaluations were based upon observing "normal" behavior in thousands of people over the course of his lifetime.

Jung believed that specific patterns, types, or combinations of preferences in humans could be described and categorized. There are opposing pairs of preferences, which he explained. A preference, according to Jung, is *the conscious or unconscious choice an individual makes in a certain designated realm.* Every individual's personality, Jung theorized, is represented by a combination of these preferences. In all, there are 16 different combinations of the preferences, each with a unique description, making up the respective Jung-Myers personality types.

This preference analysis does not involve questions of good and bad. There are no inherently superior personality types and no inferior types. Rather, Jung and later Isabel Myers pointed out major differences in people's perspectives, shedding substantial light on why people behave as they do.

Interestingly, Jung never set out to formulate a "test" of any kind. In fact, his research into typology was more of a sidelight to his mainstream study of conventional psychology. It was a series of conflicts with his mentor, Sigmund Freud, which first led Jung to consider how it was possible they saw things so differently. "In attempting to answer this question, I came across the problem of types," related Jung.[1] "For it is one's psychological type which from the outset determines and limits a person's judgment."

As Jung considered this nascent theory of "personality type," he took it further in considering the differences between himself and his wife, Emma. "There are other people who decide the same problems I have to decide, but in an entirely different way," wrote Jung.[2] "They look at things in an entirely different light, they have entirely different values." These differences, determined Jung, are accounted for by psychological types.

While Jung originated these ideas and substantiated them with the study of tens of thousands of ordinary subjects, he was not the one to push his findings into the mainstream. At one point, in fact, Jung stated that "fitting...individuals into a rigid system is 'futile'."[3]

An Ordinary Promoter

It is ironic, yet perhaps somehow appropriate that this rare psychological study of "normal" people would be popularized by a very "normal" person, herself. Isabel Myers was about the least likely person to create a personality test that one could imagine. A forty-four-year-old housewife and mother of two teenage children, Myers had zero credentials in the world of psychology.

It was her mother, Katherine Briggs, who had first taken a keen interest in the work of Dr. Carl Jung upon reading the first English translations of his *Psychological Types*. For Katherine, however, the interest was nothing more than a hobby, for the most part, as she contemplated the merits of the boy courting her daughter.

That daughter, who became Isabel Myers upon marriage, was a happy and energetic homemaker, engaged in periodic ventures into novel and play-writing. It was in January of 1942, during the early days of World War II, that Myers came upon a magazine article praising a "people-sorting instrument" used "to place the worker in the proper niche."[4] Fully aware of her mother's longtime interest in this area, Isabel excitedly wrote her mother with news of this finding.

As she set out to investigate the test that was the subject of the story, however, Myers found it to be quite unsatisfactory. Much to her surprise, upon reporting her disappointing findings back to her mother, Isabel received an unexpected reply.

Mother Briggs responded that if Isabel wanted a people-sorter that worked, perhaps she should create it herself. Her mother suggested that Myers create her own test, one based on Jung's psychological types. The energetic housewife got right to work, studying not only Jung, but anything she could find at the public library involving statistics and psychometrics. Not only did Isabel Myers develop a test inspired by Jung's work, but she even added a fourth dyad to Jung's original three.

The result became a global phenomenon. The Myers-Briggs Type Indicator (MBTI) has been translated into sixteen languages and is taken by millions of people every year. Its publisher brands it "the world's most popular personality assessment."[5]

Another Disciple

As improbable as housewife Isabel Myers becoming the one to refine Dr. Carl Jung's work and effectively promote it, the next development was no less remarkable. Jonathan Niednagel, a finance major by training, was working in a Midwestern city in the early 1970s when his employer decided to expand to the west coast, and tabbed him to head up and oversee the initial staffing of the new office.

Having no previous experience in personnel matters, Niednagel contemplated how to best assess the various applicants as he prepared to commence the hiring process. Ever the persnickety sort who paid great attention to detail and left little to chance, Niednagel determined that the optimal way to evaluate potential hires was to best understand what made them tick. He began collecting and examining psychological instruments with the hope of finding a "system" he could implement that would provide objective structure to the evaluation process.

As his investigation progressed, however, Niednagel ran into the aforementioned problem with today's commercial "personality" inventories. Most had a dubious premise or were based on abstract psychological theory. When he came across Jung's material, however, Niednagel felt he finally had something substantive on which he could rely. As a fellow keen observer of the world around him, Niednagel appreciated the fact that Jung's typology was not based on abstract theory, but rather on the painstaking observations of tens of thousands of ordinary people.

An Unwitting Discovery

After staffing his office, Niednagel found he did not leave his newfound interest in assessing people behind. In fact, it continued to grow. "I began to notice things in people and thought, *wow, I can even apply this*," related Niednagel.[6] From the workplace to social functions, to even interacting with a stranger on the street, Niednagel began to sense that he could quickly discern clues as to Jung's original findings on what made up the inner-person. Even that realization, however, would not prepare Niednagel for what he was about to discover.

He shared the story of his revelation in a later interview: "As it progressed more and more, the next thing I knew, I started coaching my children in their sports teams, and as I noticed little kids moving a certain way with certain kinds of personalities, I thought, this is really bizarre. It's one thing to say this little boy is a sensate because he can't take this concept at all. It's another thing to say this sensing, feeling boy is using the big muscles of his body just like that other sensing, feeling boy over there! How come this abstract, thinking boy doesn't use the big muscles at all, but just uses nothing but his wrists? And yet so does this other conceptual, thinking boy—he does the same thing!

As I began to weigh these different kids and their behaviors as (Gregor) Mendel did his pea plants, I realized that something's got to be going on here that is beyond what I see. There's something inside, and it probably has something to do with genetics."[7]

An(other) Amateur Ascertainment

Gregor Mendel, of course, was another unwitting pioneer who made a landmark discovery far outside his trained field of work. Mendel was an Austrian monk whose *hobby* was botany—the study of plants. In the mid-1860s, Mendel conducted meticulous experiments on plant life—specifically pea plants. Over a seven-year period, Mendel studied nearly 30,000 pea plants.

As Mendel carefully manipulated the manner in which he cultivated the pea plants, he was able only to observe the results from inspecting the outside of the plant. However, he realized that something must be taking place *inside* the plants in order to produce what he was observing on the *outside*. Mendel had deduced the principles of genetics!

As author Nancy Andreasen writes, "We can summarize Mendel's observations and conclusions by using modern terminology. Mendel was observing the phenotype, but behind the phenotype was a genotype... Mendel could not see the genotype—only the phenotype. Nonetheless, he inferred the presence of something that must represent a genotype, since this was the most plausible explanation of the patterns of transmission that he was observing."[8]

Though it had long been observed that certain traits, such as eye color, hair color, etc. are transmitted within families, Mendel's principles of heredity were scientifically rejected at the time they were revealed. Only decades after he died did his theories become widely accepted. Today, Austrian monk and amateur botanist Gregor Mendel is considered by many to be the "father of modern genetics."

The Search Begins

Niednagel continues: "So I went and got some brain books and started reading. Is there anything that regulates our motor skills? I also went off to libraries and, especially when I started studying more of the brain, I went off to medical libraries. I even contacted some brain imaging centers. I contacted some neuroscientists and said, 'I have an interest in this…'

One of the teams I coached had a father who was a neuroscientist at the university, and I happened to talk to him about this. He said, 'Well, Jon, there's a primary motor cortex of the brain and it controls voluntary motor skills, and sure the cerebellum does too, for balance and all, but why don't you check that out?'

And, sure enough, I started seeing these different segments of the brain relating to the various motor skills. So, I started to make this connection between motor skills and personality…"[9]

As his two sons grew, Niednagel would proceed to coach upwards of fifty amateur sports teams from the peewee level up through high school. As a coach, not only was he able to carefully evaluate and develop each player on his team(s), but he was able to view and monitor the thousands of youngsters against whom they competed. The appearance of each child, as well as the manner in which the child moved and behaved, provided quick and discernible clues as to his or her specific innate wiring.

Word Spreads

As Niednagel effectively utilized his new acumen to identify and develop young athletes, it brought remarkable success to his youth coaching. Word of mouth and ensuing media exposure brought attention from many sources, all the way up to the professional ranks. Niednagel soon found himself sharing his insight with teams and athletes at both the collegiate and professional levels. Working as a consultant for teams at the highest levels of professional basketball, baseball, and football, Niednagel was able to evaluate upwards of a thousand top athletes every year, especially as they performed prior to the annual drafts in each sport. The NFL Combine, NBA pre-draft camps and MLB pre-draft workouts provided venues where the greatest young athletes in the world were brought together in one location for workouts. It provided a marvelous laboratory for Niednagel to further explore this relationship between "personality" and motor skills.

Over three plus decades of conducting this meticulous empirical research, Niednagel estimates that he studied over 50,000 people. That is in addition to the countless others he observed in passing, providing further reinforcement and affirmation of his findings. Just as Mendel did more than a century prior, Niednagel inferred what was going on inside by what he observed on the outside of people.

Put to the Test

In the early 1990s, Niednagel was put to the test by renowned sports scientist, Vic Braden. Not only was Braden a legendary tennis coach, but he was also a licensed psychologist, and to say he was skeptical of Niednagel's findings would be an understatement. Braden was so leery of these claims, in fact, that he constructed a "test" at his tennis academy with which he intended to disprove Niednagel's theory. The test involved one hundred subjects and took place over the course of more than a year. Niednagel would meet each test subject (for the first time) and conduct a brief face-to-face interview. He was not permitted to ask any questions about their athletic abilities or to observe their body movements beyond the interview. Following the interview, Niednagel would share with the subject a detailed rundown on his or her athletic proficiencies, weaknesses, tendencies, and off-the-court behavior, based only on his interview. He would also tell Braden how each subject would perform on the tennis court or in any other physical exercise in which they engaged.

According to the stunned Braden, Niednagel aced the test, repeatedly amazing both his skeptic and the individual subjects with his insights. Some test subjects even declared that Niednagel knew them better than they knew themselves. In fact, one of the subjects in the study was a Ph.D. research scientist, who was reticent to comment for professional reasons, yet admitted Niednagel was "remarkably and disturbingly accurate."[10] Needless to say, Niednagel had gained a supporter for life in the effervescent Braden.

While conventional personality tests mandate that the subject answer a multitude of questions, how was Niednagel able to pull off his feat with just a brief interview? Even more remarkable, how was he able to make the motor skill determinations? One clue is because the human face is composed of over 40 muscles. As you read and consider the information in this book, you will understand how these underlying muscles can provide substantive and useful clues as to the genetic makeup of the underlying person.

As stated earlier, "personality" to the layperson conveys the sum total of the mental, emotional, and social characteristics of an individual. The term "personality," however, originates from the Latin word "persona." It corresponds to the Greek word for face. Actors in ancient Greece could perform more than one role on stage by donning different personas or

masks. One's innate behavior, on the other hand, is not dictated primarily by the faces we randomly choose to wear, but by our genetic "framework" primarily (but not exclusively) manifested and orchestrated in the brain.

Modern-Day Science Boosting Long-Held Theory

Niednagel did not "invent" any of his theory. He simply built upon the empirical data collected by Jung and his subsequent protagonists by applying the latest neuroscientific, genetic, biomechanic, and vision-related findings. Niednagel's goal was to take Jung's "soft" typological findings into the 21st century "hard" sciences for verification. These efforts left him with no doubt that Jung (and his modern-day devotees) was (and are) on the right track. However, they remain far removed from the accuracy and scientific understanding now available for evaluating human behavior (cognitive, physical, and spatial).

Not only did Niednagel believe that Jung's original "type" preferences and functions can be attributed to specific regions of the brain, but they can be directly linked to specific motor and spatial skills, especially via the brain's motor cortex. Whereas Jung's followers and others in the field have devoted their attentions to outward "personality" characteristics, Niednagel's studies and experience led him to dig deeper. His mission was to minimize outward persona and focus instead on internal biological and physical characteristics that dictate cognitive, physical, and spatial behaviors. Niednagel was most interested in the quantifiable and verifiable physiological behavioral dimensions—to be applied pragmatically to living life.

Though personas can vary significantly within individuals of each design (due to nurture—parenting, upbringing, etc., and nature—genetic variances, etc.), Niednagel's research led him to an undeniable conclusion:

---

*Differing inborn neural networks in each design affect specific cognitive, physical, and spatial skills, and similarities within each design are due to **genetic hardwiring—nature**.*

Deciphering the Message

Jonathan Niednagel amazed people with the insights from his discovery and his remarkable ability to discern individual inborn designs for years. Unfortunately, the same innate hardwiring that both enabled Niednagel to make this discovery and to expertly distinguish the nuances in people also hampered his ability to effectively share it with others. Though he has consulted for over two dozen major league sports teams and countless other organizations and individuals over the years, time and again he quickly wore out his welcome at each stop. The problem in each case was his inability to effectively convey how this information might be useful beyond the initial personnel issue he was brought in to address.

Though few could fully grasp what Niednagel did or how he did it, there was never a shortage of referrals. Once with a new organization, however, only those who took great pains to understand could effectively begin to grasp the full meaning of Niednagel's insights, such was the convoluted manner in which he tended to share his discovery. As a top executive with the Cincinnati Reds, I was one of those select few.

Unique Perspective

In the winter of 2000-2001, the Reds were in the midst of a difficult high-profile managerial search. We had just fired a popular manager and were under great scrutiny from fans and the media as we went through the process of hiring a replacement. Leaving no stone unturned in our pursuit, we explored every avenue we could find for insights and information on perspective candidates. When my boss got the Niednagel referral from a fellow MLB executive, he jumped at the opportunity to bring in a different perspective. Now, when I say different, I mean *dif-fer-ENT!*

After a brief one-on-one interview with each of the three finalists in our search, Niednagel was ready to share his insights with the 12-member managerial search committee. In the old-school, tobacco-spitting world of baseball, to say Niednagel's presentation was unique would be quite an understatement. As the room sat listening in perplexed silence, Niednagel was drawing diagrams of the brain on the board and telling us how the mind of each candidate functioned.

I scribbled notes feverishly as I attempted to follow along and grasp where this soft-spoken stranger was coming from. To our amazement, though the details of his process seemed to be explained in a foreign language, the substance of his analysis was right on the mark!

Two of the finalists were well-known by members of the search committee, as they were internal candidates. We had become aware of their tendencies and mannerisms through first-person interactions and close observation. Yet here was this outsider sharing insights from a brief meeting that had taken us years to gain! In addition, Niednagel shared a revelation in regard to the third candidate, who had really impressed the committee by being largely in tune with our way of thinking. Niednagel explained that it made sense we could relate best to the third candidate's mindset and perspective, because he shared the same innate wiring as most members of the committee!

After Niednagel left town, my boss and I agreed that we needed to explore this—*whatever it is*—further. He instructed me to negotiate a consulting contract and appointed me the chief liaison, coordinating Niednagel's assignments and facilitating the flow of useful information from his insights.

Useful at Work *and* Home

As Director of the first formal Research and Development department in MLB, I was thrilled to have this opportunity to explore a potentially revolutionary method for discerning the internal drive of players—what we referred to as "makeup." What I quickly found, however, was not only did I gain useful insight when it came to baseball personnel, but it was extremely helpful with my family, as well.

This new insight gave me a better understanding of—and *appreciation* for—my wonderful, loving wife. It allowed me to see clearly the special way she loved me and all that she did for our marriage, including much I had not appreciated properly before, if I had even noticed at all. Best of all, it enabled me to realize and fully appreciate her inner beauty. No longer were any disagreements a matter of right and wrong so much as a difference of perspective. I found that I was able to better quantify and cherish the perspective she brought to our relationship.

The benefits at home did not stop with my wife. I also gained insights for better relating to our young children—especially our son, who was quite a handful for us. I could see that he was different from me—very different—in some ways I considered good and others that may not be so good. As I came to understand the way he was innately designed, I was able to quantify those differences and gain a more constructive comprehension of my son's behavioral tendencies, as neither inherently "good" or "bad," but simply different. In addition, I was able to formulate an effective strategy for being the best father I could be.

Perhaps most importantly, it was a revelation for understanding myself. I had always possessed what I considered to be pretty high self-esteem, but I wasn't always satisfied with my performance. I also regretted my behavior at times. This new insight finally provided an understandable basis for not only why I had certain feelings, but also why I behaved and performed as I did—not just in athletics, but in the classroom, in the office, and at home. My life would never be the same.

Niednagel consulted for the Reds for three years, during which time we traveled the country together. Just as Vic Braden had done years before, I frequently put Niednagel to the test. Whether evaluating potential players we hoped to acquire or refining the talent of players who were already in our organization, Niednagel's insights provided a remarkably useful perspective. We made exciting progress during that time, exploring avenues by which this new technology could be utilized to gain a significant competitive advantage. Unfortunately, internal politics terminated this revolutionary exploration prematurely.

Spreading the Word

I left major league baseball a few years later, in large part because of my desire to further my knowledge of this remarkable new behavioral science. I was also driven by the insight that I was gifted in ways Niednagel was not. I was confident I could help him with a skill that was outside his innate area of giftedness—sharing this discovery with others. For the greater part of the next decade, I would be Niednagel's understudy and chief advisor, assisting with research projects of all kinds, as well as conducting educational seminars and designing related material to help others benefit from this knowledge.

Sadly, just as we were closing in on the completion of several projects designed to share this discovery with the masses, Niednagel was hit with a debilitating illness that sapped his energy and effectively derailed our efforts. As Niednagel turned his laser-like focus to health-related concerns, it became apparent that it would be left to me if this amazing revelation was to be shared with the world in a meaningful way.

User Friendly Guidebook

As I mentioned, even prior to Niednagel's illness, we faced a significant problem when it came to sharing this breakthrough in human understanding. Quite simply, Niednagel's propensity for excruciating detail, while a positive for research purposes, left the explanation rather difficult for others to easily grasp. As I venture forth to share these insights, my overriding goal is to do it in a format that will make it easiest to learn and implement—for everyone.

The information contained in this book reveals a revolutionary method of human understanding, along with a system for utilizing it that is remarkably simple. Just as each person is hardwired at conception for certain traits, such as hair color, eye color, handedness, etc., we are also pre-programmed for a specific manner of behavior and performance. Though many clues are provided via our day-to-day personality, our environment often shapes the way we act and behave, which is why there is so much confusion in the personality assessment industry.

Supporting information has been provided where necessary and helpful for better comprehension, but potentially confusing minutiae is purposely absent wherever possible. The purpose of this book is not to *prove* this revolutionary behavioral science to doubters who refuse to objectively consider the evidence. Rather, it is intended as an easy-to-use guide from which *everyone* can realize life-changing benefits similar to what I experienced. As you consider these insights, you will find that humans, while complex beings, are designed in a remarkably orderly fashion.

The Beginning of the Rest of Your Life

Every area of your life that involves people will benefit from the understanding you are about to gain. The way you look at both yourself and others will never be the same. Not only will you achieve a new understanding of your inherent giftedness and capabilities, but you will acquire a more substantive realization and acceptance of your relative limitations. In addition, you will realize increased appreciation for the different perspectives, behaviors, and performance of others.

Not only is this unchanging circuitry from conception our driving force *for our entire lifetime*, but it is also the engine that drives our persona, behavior and performance as we live our lives. Both for the way we live and for as long as we live, each and every one of us is *hardwired for life!*

Part I

INTELLIGENT(LY) DESIGNED

1

An Intelligent Design

Have you ever wondered why you do the things you do? Why you naturally think, feel, and behave a certain way? Have you ever felt frustrated with the way you are and wished you could be different? Not your outward appearance, so much, but rather the way you feel inside. Have you ever believed you should think or act in a particular manner, yet you feel naturally inclined otherwise?

How about athletically? Growing up, did you ever wish you could perform in a certain way, yet frustratingly wonder why you struggled, regardless of how much you practiced? Did you ever wonder why some things seemed to come naturally, while others required so much more effort?

I experienced that bewilderment, which only grew as I observed and interacted with others. One vivid memory is playing tennis with my future wife and wondering how we could play the game so differently in every way. From tactics to motor skills, we approached the game with a stark contrast in styles. As a high-energy competitor, I considered myself the better "athlete," aggressively racing around the court. Yet she was calmly the superior player, pounding me into submission with "boring," yet consistent and accurate ground strokes. *What gives*, I asked myself? Years later, I learned the information I am about to share with you and, finally, it all made sense!

You are Special, but How?

"God made you special..."

"Appreciate your special gifts..."

"Use your special talents..."

We have all said or heard statements similar to these in some form or another, but what do we mean? So often we say or hear these forms of general encouragement, yet we are unable to apply the specifics. How can we quantify this feeling that we have or are at least *supposed* to have? Why do we feel compelled to keep repeating these statements, or the need to hear them over and over? It probably has something to do with the fact that in many cases we are unable to put our finger on what it is we feel or what we are talking about—until now! This remarkable methodology will enable you to finally identify and understand specifically how each person, including yourself, is specifically designed to have a special, high-level intelligence.

Each person in the world is, indeed, specially gifted in some specific way. Unfortunately, this also means we are each born with certain inherent limitations. By gaining an understanding of both our strengths and weaknesses, however, we become better equipped to navigate life's journey.

Often we act, or *react* to situations without even consciously contemplating our actions in advance, only to look back with wonder. You are about to learn how your brain is hardwired from conception to give you a predisposition toward a certain persona, as well as related inherent behaviors and performance capabilities. You will also learn how you possess the equivalent of a "genius"-level I.Q. in your specific area of innate giftedness. First, consider how different attributes might impact certain situations in their own unique, yet vital ways.

The Nature of the Task

Have you ever asked a child (or someone smaller than you) to try to reach something because your hand was too large to get through a small opening? Or maybe you asked somebody with stronger hands to open a jar. Perhaps you can recall a tall person being able to reach a high shelf or an overhead fixture. In the same way, a shorter person might be able to more easily navigate around and through low-hanging branches along a wooded nature trail. It all depends on the nature of the task at hand in order to determine what characteristic(s), skill(s), or talent(s) are most desired.

Consider another admittedly simplified, yet representative example. A group of people needs to cut a large quantity of paper, but the group only has left-handed scissors at its disposal. What trait would suddenly become of primary importance? Would it make sense to simply pick someone at random to do the cutting, or might it be beneficial to inquire if anyone in the group is naturally *left-handed*? Once again, the important innate strength or "giftedness" to be considered is directly related to the nature of the task at hand or the issue(s) being dealt with. Even the fastest "scissor-cutter" in town might be of little use in this instance if primarily right-hand dominant. In this situation, relatively uncommon "handedness" is obviously a helpful trait to identify among members of the group.

Same but Different

While on the topic of "handedness," think about exactly what that means. What is the difference between someone who is "right-handed" and someone who is "left-handed"? Both people have two hands, but they are each naturally hardwired to be more proficient with one hand over the other.

Perhaps you know of people who are relatively proficient with both hands. Even in those instances, however, most tend to naturally favor one hand over the other for certain specific tasks. What you are about to learn in this book will be easier to comprehend if you keep in mind the concept of "handedness." That is, most people have two perfectly functioning hands, yet tend to be more adept and comfortable using one in particular.

Who is "Gifted"?

Identifying "gifted" young people has become an increasingly popular objective in schools across the U.S., but what are these programs really identifying? Merriam-Webster's dictionary defines the term gifted as "having great natural ability." Schools, understandably, interpret this natural ability to be with regard to academic areas, most specifically math and science. There is an increasing movement to label children who show proficiency in these academic areas, segregating them into exclusive "gifted" programs.

While I don't begrudge the efforts and desire to enhance the "giftedness" of students who display these specific skills and abilities, I am more concerned about the remaining young people. For those who may not be identified as "gifted," what should they consider themselves? *Un*-gifted? *Un*-talented?? *Disappointing*???

What if we could objectively identify some way in which *every* child is *gifted*? Will it not be a better world the day our schools and our society can objectively and tangibly identify and celebrate the giftedness of each student and every person? We could all then be guided in programs to accentuate and enhance our innate giftedness. Well, I have good news. That time is now!

Congratulations, You're A Genius!

The fact is, everyone—including yourself—possesses the potential for a "genius"-level I.Q.—in his or her (or your) particular area of *giftedness*. Unfortunately, due to the manner in which people are often labeled in today's computer-based society, this genius is usually thought to be someone in the technical or scientific sense. Consider the sayings we use every day to describe projects that do not require genius-level intelligence. *It's not rocket science! It's not brain surgery!* In other words, to most people, being "gifted" denotes the ability to perform a task involving a high-level technical or scientific basis.

Even when it comes to measuring "genius" in adults, the conventional standard is to base it on an I.Q. test. Have you ever considered who *designs* I.Q. tests and other measures of "giftedness"? People *hardwired* in a manner to score high on such a profile, of course.

Have you ever considered that someone with a high "emotional I.Q." might be a "genius"? In a world full of *people*, would it not make sense to place value on those who have an innate proficiency for inter-personal relations and communication?

Open your mind to the world we live in. Consider the people in your life and their various perspectives on certain issues. Think of areas where you may have had a disagreement with somebody— perhaps your spouse, a friend, or a co-worker. Rather than one of you being "right" and the other "wrong," is it possible that each of you is simply hardwired in a way that leads you to see the situation differently? Now, keep in mind, this is *not* to say that one of you does not have a more optimal perspective on the matter. The insights provided by comprehending how everyone is hardwired will help to consider that another person may very well have a better perspective on a particular issue.

Let me provide an illustration that reveals how this might be so. Pick out a book that has a detailed title description on the front cover and nothing on the back. Stand the book upright on a table and imagine several people sitting around the book in a circle. Each person is looking at the book from his or her unique angle. Now, change seats and describe what you see from another person's perspective. Each sees the same book differently from his or her vantage point. No one is wrong in describing the book, but some have a better angle to optimally comprehend the contents of the book. This is who we should rely upon for the most accurate description in this case. The others are not necessarily incorrect or inaccurate in describing what they see; they simply cannot see enough to give a comprehensive perspective, though their insights may still have value.

It is similar to the tale of the blind men and the elephant, popularized by 19th century American poet John Godfrey Saxe. Six blind men all feel different specific parts of the elephant, including the trunk, tusk, ear, side, leg, and tail. As they discuss their findings, each confident of his newfound knowledge, a heated dispute predictably ensues. The poem ends:

> *Each in his own opinion,*
> *Exceeding stiff and strong,*
> *Though each was partly in the right,*
> *And all were in the wrong!* [11]

These analogies are both relevant to the various ways each of us is uniquely and specifically hardwired with an inborn neural circuitry. Each person is especially gifted to perceive and judge matters according to his or her unique cerebral design. Everyone possesses inherent "strengths" and "weaknesses," be they mental, emotional, physical, or some combination thereof, yet there has never been a way to comprehensively quantify this—until now. This new system of human understanding illuminates the inherent strengths and weaknesses in every person, allowing us to identify, celebrate, and benefit from *true* behavioral and performance diversity.

Vital Importance

With over 2,500 hundred different versions of personality "tests" on the market, it might be easy to conclude there is no need to throw another one on the pile. That is precisely why this information is so important for anyone concerned with accurately understanding people.

Despite marketing promises to the contrary, most conventional personality tests reveal little tangible or actionable information about the test subject. This is in part because the results are clouded by the impact of the "nurture" variable. One of the most common hardwired designs, especially, can have an extremely varied persona, due to environmental factors, as well as subtle genetic variances.

This flaw in commercial personality testing is a major reason why these tests are extremely unreliable and of dubious utility. For one thing, questions in these tests can be interpreted differently by different people, due to education, cultural differences, etc. In addition, the variances within each hardwired design mean that very few people fall cleanly into the groupings designated by these tests.

Even the most popular commercial personality test, the MBTI, has a history of extreme unreliability. Several studies have revealed that over half of MBTI test takers come up with a different personality type when taking the test a second time. One study even found that a similar degree of variance can occur within a few weeks![12] How useful can any measurement device really be that has such a significant margin of error? The fact is, any arbitrary group of questions can easily lead to dubious conclusions.

The Difference-Making Motor Skills Connection

What makes the discovery of hardwired designs in people so significant is the unmistakable body skill correlation. The fact that motor skill proficiency directly correlates with behavior and performance potential provides us with a perspective that gets to the core of each person. It also relegates questionnaires to being little more than a supplementary tool for solving the human understanding puzzle.

The remarkable motor skills correlation provides tangible and unequivocal clues that can serve to either reinforce or call into question the initial impression provided by perfunctory question-and-answer investigation. In many cases, motor skill-related physical clues can provide even more information about a person's inborn hardwired design than any answers to arbitrary questions. This is why a person-to-person interaction can quickly reveal so much. Hardwiring methodology provides a mechanism for quantifying the information that many of us consciously—and subconsciously—gather already.

Help for Self

Gaining an understanding of how each person is innately hardwired will help you to understand and appreciate both yourself and others more fully. Most importantly, by accurately identifying your own inborn design, you will gain a new perspective regarding why your brain works as it does—why you view matters and make decisions as you do. You will be able to ascertain aspects of yourself that you always wanted to know, yet could never figure out. Yet the insights are not limited to the mental aspect. Presented with the physical motor skill perspective, you will gain new appreciation for what you are *naturally* capable of doing athletically and to what degree.

In addition, you will acquire increased awareness of why you tend to regard others as you do socially. Not only will you achieve this new clarity of self-understanding, but you will realize increased comprehension of why other people in your life think, behave, and perform as they do. You will better appreciate and relate to your spouse, your children, your friends, your neighbors, your coworkers—virtually everyone in your life!

Best of all, once properly versed in this new method of human understanding, the insights can be implemented with virtually every person you meet in just *minutes*! Finally, you can employ an objective technique founded on the latest advances in the hard sciences to deal with the subjective world of people.

Who Am I? Who Are You?

We already contemplated if you have ever wondered why you do the things you do or feel the way you feel? Now, take a step back and look into the proverbial mirror. How well do you know yourself? Why do you walk, talk, and think the way you do? Why do you have your particular likes and dislikes? What motivates you, and why? For what reason do you seem to naturally excel in some areas while you perpetually struggle in others?

Perhaps you have pondered why others behave as they do, or maybe even how they are able to perform in such a way? Have you ever wondered why you seem to "click" with certain people, yet others just seem to rub you the wrong way? Perhaps you have struggled to relate to or get along with your boss or coworkers. Or maybe you are a parent who is waging a battle to better understand children who not only behave and perform very differently from each other, but often seem to be nothing like you.

Think about even the closest and most important relationship—that between husband and wife, two people who made an original commitment to remain together through thick and thin, for better, for worse, for richer, for poorer, in sickness and in health, until separated only by death. Of almost a million divorces taking place in the United States every year, well over half of these "lifetime" partnerships dissolve prematurely because of what is termed "irreconcilable differences." How many of these "differences" might be dealt with effectively if each spouse simply understood the other better—at a more fundamental level?

By opening up this ground-breaking book, you have started down the road to realizing answers that previously seemed unfathomable. You will learn that there *is* an objective and tangible way to better understand yourself, your spouse, your children, and anyone else in your life. This will become possible as you learn to comprehend the specific manner in which each person's brain has been hardwired at conception. The design of this specific cerebral circuitry predisposes every person throughout life to certain identifiable talents, behaviors, and dispositions.

2

Hardwired Body Skills

Every person employs a pair of basic mental functions as we live life. First we PERCEIVE something. Then we give it THOUGHT. For each of these, we have two different and distinct methods of implementation.

Perception is attained either by *observing* ("what is") or *imagining* ("what could be"). Next, we incorporate thought in order to determine how we value what was perceived. For instance, we might decide if we like it or dislike it, and to what degree. We do this in either a *personal* (emotional) or *impersonal* (unemotional) fashion. Every person is specifically hardwired from birth to use these four cerebral functions in very specific ways, depending upon his or her individually designed circuitry.

Of course, we all perceive with both "observation" and "imagination" to some degree, just as we all think on both a "personal" as well as "impersonal" basis. However, we are each hardwired from conception to be strongest in—and thus, naturally favor—one realm over the other. The manifestations of these may be impacted, sometimes significantly, due to our "nurturing."

Consider the various dimensions of "perception" and "thought":

PERCEPTION

OBSERVE
- Empirical
- Five Senses
- "What Is"
- Reality
- Facts
- Concrete
- Pragmatic
- Tangible
- Details ("trees")

IMAGINE
- Conceptual
- "Sixth Sense"
- "What Could Be"
- Possibility
- Dreams
- Abstract
- Visionary
- Intangible
- Big Picture ("forest")

THOUGHT

PERSONAL
- Empathetic
- Animate World
- Feeling
- Caring
- People
- Subjective
- Emotional
- Harmony

IMPERSONAL
- Analytic
- Inanimate World
- Thinking
- Logic
- Things
- Objective
- Matter-of-Fact
- Principle

As you proceed through this material, think about yourself, as well as other people you know well. You will learn techniques and steps for properly identifying the innate hardwiring of yourselves and others.

Interchanging the various combinations, we see that each person is pre-programmed at conception—by individual genetics—to be most (and least) adept in one—and only one—of four possible mindsets:

1) Observe Personally

2) Observe Impersonally

3) Imagine Personally

4) Imagine Impersonally

In considering these combinations, a good place to start is to see if you can identify a combination that the person in question definitely *is not*. If you can do that, there is a good chance the subject is actually the *opposite*. Of course, as discussed in the introduction, most of us can don the appropriate "mask" and take on the desired persona when relaxed and properly focused, particularly if we have learned to do so (nurture). Therefore, it is imperative to consider how the subjects feels or behaves when experiencing "pressure" of some sort, such as when facing a deadline. This reveals more accurately how one is *hardwired* to function, as opposed to how one may have *learned* to operate.

By discovering which combination of the four listed above represents you (and others) most to the least, a new world of human understanding will be revealed. Within each of these four broad areas of mental giftedness (observing or imagining either personally or impersonally), there are four unique inborn designs. This results in a total of sixteen specific and exclusive hardwired combinations. Every human being is born with a specific version of one—and only one—of these unique designs. Although we undergo neurological/chemical changes as our brains age, this specific neural circuitry is hardwired (similar to "handedness") in each of us for a lifetime!

Here is where things get especially exciting. Not only does each design have a unique mental makeup, but each one correlates with a specific physical/motor proficiency. This revelation means that all people the world over can, for the first time, be individually identified, appreciated, and nurtured in almost the same way as have many species of animals and plants!

Hardwiring Takes Us Behind the Mask

As discussed earlier, one of the problems associated with most all "personality" and psychological assessment methodologies in use today is that they seek to identify unscientific "personality" nuances. Hardwiring is the only methodology based on specific inborn cognitive and motor functions. Other approaches are not only unreliable, but they use subjectively answered questionnaires to reach their conclusions. With these methods, the subject can essentially appear however they choose to see themselves, as opposed to identifying who they *truly* are from a more objective perspective.

Other approaches, at best, serve only to identify the personality nuances accumulated over one's lifetime. They mix the effects of nurture with one's inborn nature, leaving them woefully unequipped to identify the true inborn person. With no basis in the hard sciences, other methods fail to describe anything beyond an outward persona— the mask that each of us *chooses* to wear.

Put On the "Good Face"

Have you ever prepared to attend a function—like a business meeting or a social gathering—where you considered it beneficial to display a certain "persona"? Perhaps you felt the need to "lay down the law" in your business meeting, so you made a point to display a "tough" persona. Or, maybe you were going to an important party that you would rather have been skipping, so you knew you had to make it a point to be proactively engaging and pleasant.

Even spur-of-the-moment, one-on-one encounters may lead us to wear a specific "mask" for the intention at hand. We have all approached a clerk in a store or called customer service at some point, looking for help or demanding satisfaction, consciously tailoring our persona, accordingly.

Most of us learn early in life that it is beneficial to *act* in a certain way when it comes to dealing with others, as we see that specific behaviors and manners may increase the odds of obtaining a desired outcome. Even an interaction as simple as paying for a soda at a convenience store is impacted by the way we *act*. Someone who naturally *imagines impersonally*, thereby normally more aloof, can make it a point to "act" nice and engaging during the brief interaction in order to increase the odds of it being a pleasant encounter.

Gaming the Test

Now, consider sitting down to take a conventional "personality test" for the purpose of getting hired for a job. Perhaps it could be for counseling (e.g., marital, parental, anger management, etc.) or another third-party evaluation of some kind. Would it not make sense that we would want to "put our best foot forward" in such a situation? I am not suggesting outright lies, mind you, but rather making every effort to show ourselves in the best light possible. In other words, we will select the best "mask" we can reasonably wear in order to achieve what we believe to be the desired objective of the test.

How about a casual "personality test" that we take just for fun? Even there we may subconsciously deceive ourselves. It is not unlike looking in the mirror and seeing what we "want" to see. All too often, the way we see ourselves is different from the way we appear to others who know us well.

Understanding how people are uniquely and specifically hardwired, along with insights regarding how to detect it, will make these misreads a thing of the past.

The Body Skills Connection

The key to eliminating misreads is the fact that the way someone is hardwired impacts not only their persona and behavior, but also their motor skills—in a direct correlation. Interestingly, this motor skill proficiency area also happens to coincide with four basic physical stages of development through which all humans progress as they grow toward puberty. Each of these physical stages are crucial for living a normal, healthy life. The four stages develop in the following order:

1) **Gross**-motor, or the large-muscle groups
2) FINE-motor, or the small muscles of the hand region
3) **Mouth** region—muscles that control speech, etc.
4) *Diaphragm* region—muscles that control voice, air flow, etc.

Which is most important? It depends, of course, upon what you need to do. Just as with the exaggerated examples provided in chapter one, if you needed someone to operate a left-handed pair of scissors, the most important body skill in that situation would be *left-handed proficiency*.

Similar to modes of perception and thought, each person is particularly skilled in one—and only one—of these four muscle groupings. Every person uses all four, of course, and can become quite adept in more than one, but we are each born to be most skilled in only one. This is our most proficient natural physical skill and will remain so throughout our lives, even if we fail to develop it to an expert level. Remarkably, all who are most innately adept in each of these physical areas also share inborn mental and cognitive similarities with others who are hardwired with a similar body skill proficiency.

The Motor Cortex

Every person's voluntary motor movements are made possible due to a narrow strip called the primary motor cortex that runs along the surface of the brain. This vital strip runs from the inside of each hemisphere, over the top, and then down the outside. When we move any body part, such as a hand/arm/leg, it is possible due to this portion of the brain. Each section of the motor cortex (little more than an inch or so) controls different major muscle groups. Interestingly, some of the smallest muscles in the body take up some of the largest portions of the motor cortex.

The parts of the body controlled by the primary motor cortex run in an orderly fashion, beginning with our toes at the base of the motor cortex, located at the beginning of the strip, just inside each hemisphere. Then come the feet, followed by the ankle, moving up through our core in an orderly fashion until it gets to our shoulders. The body parts controlled by the motor cortex proceed down our arms and out to our fingers before picking back up with the neck and moving into the head. The many small muscles in our face and head encompass a relatively large portion of the motor cortex, as can be seen in this generalized diagram.

As you probably know if you have studied the brain at all, the human brain is cross-wired. That is, the motor cortex on the left hemisphere is responsible for controlling the corresponding muscles on the right side of our body. Conversely, the right motor cortex controls the left side muscles.

Primary Motor Cortex

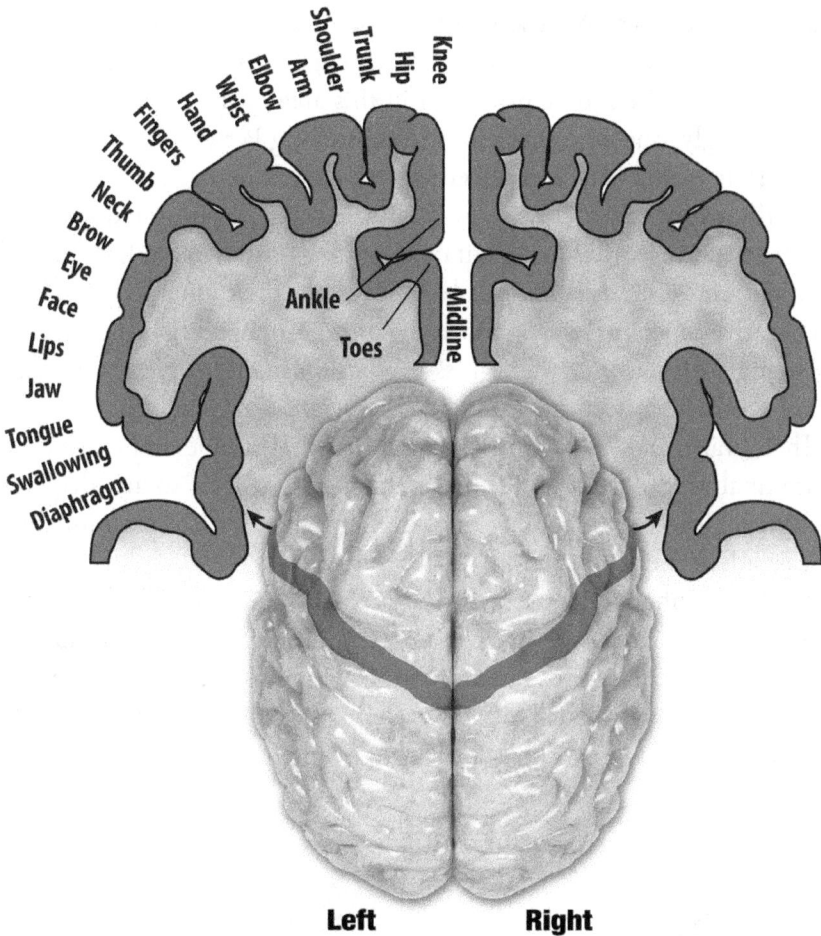

Shoulder
Trunk
Elbow
Arm
Hip
Wrist
Knee
Hand
Fingers
Thumb
Neck
Brow
Eye
Face
Lips
Jaw
Tongue
Swallowing
Diaphragm

Ankle
Toes
Midline

Left   Right

The Growth Process

What is the first thing a baby does after it leaves the mother's womb and enters the world? Most healthy babies immediately express *emotion* (by crying) and begin to *observe* the world around them soon after. The newborn uses its senses of sight, hearing, taste, touch, and smell, quickly responding to each *emotionally*. (Does this sound like any hardwired design discussed so far?) As the baby begins to move, what are the first motor skills it masters? The big muscles, of course! Any mother can attest that "landmark" days in each baby's development are marked by learning to roll over, crawl, and finally get up and walk!

I. Gross Motors

It should be no surprise that the motor skills a baby first masters are the ones located closest to the base of the motor cortex, and at the center of the brain. It would also make perfect sense that every person hardwired to be proficient in this area of the motor cortex is, accordingly, one who specializes in Observing Personally!

That is precisely what Niednagel found as he began to consider his discovery more closely. Each and every gross-motor dominant person in the world has a mental design that—above all other areas of cognition—Observes Personally! Conversely, their inherently weakest cognitive capacity is the opposite, of course—Imagining Impersonally. No matter how much these gross-motor dominant people try, they are not abstract, conceptual thinkers or logicians—nor will they ever be. Their brains are simply hardwired differently. This does not mean they are unable to develop these lesser functions, at least to an adequate degree. However, Imagining Impersonally will always be their innately least adept mental function.

Their inherent mastery of the gross motors means that people hardwired with this design will always naturally incorporate the big muscles into body movements. From swinging a golf club or tennis racket to throwing a ball to even sweeping the kitchen floor, all people sharing this design will rely primarily on the large-muscle groups of

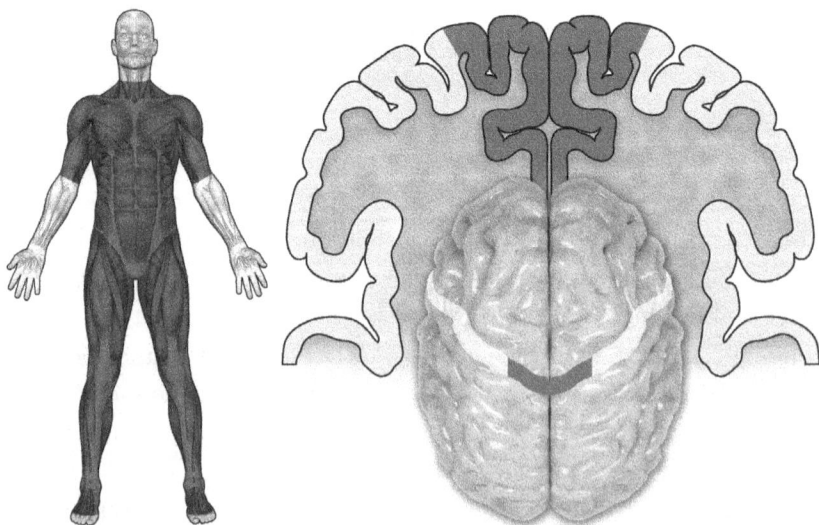

the body. Many of those born with gross-motor adeptness excel in athletics, some even reaching the highest ranks. The NBA's **LeBron James**, **Kevin Durant**, and **Kobe Bryant**, as well as baseball's **Albert Pujols**, **Miguel Cabrera**, and **Ken Griffey, Jr.** are all superstars who share this big-muscle giftedness. Of course, all gross-motor dominant people can excel in certain non-athletic vocations and hobbies, as well, where they will rely more on their innate *mental* giftedness as opposed to physical attributes.

II. Fine Motors

Back to considering how a child grows, as a baby moves into the toddler stage, it continues to reside in the world of its five senses, yet it now begins to consider and respond to observations much differently. The baby begins to remove emotion and now engages and processes issues and sensations more objectively and thoughtfully, especially in the spatial or visual realm. From picking up a toy to throwing a ball, the young child begins to consider and comprehend angles and depth perception.

Now incorporating all five senses, the toddler especially excels with its sense of sight, which it uses more than any other. At this stage, each child is learning the skills of Observing Impersonally.

Not coincidentally, as we work our way down the primary motor

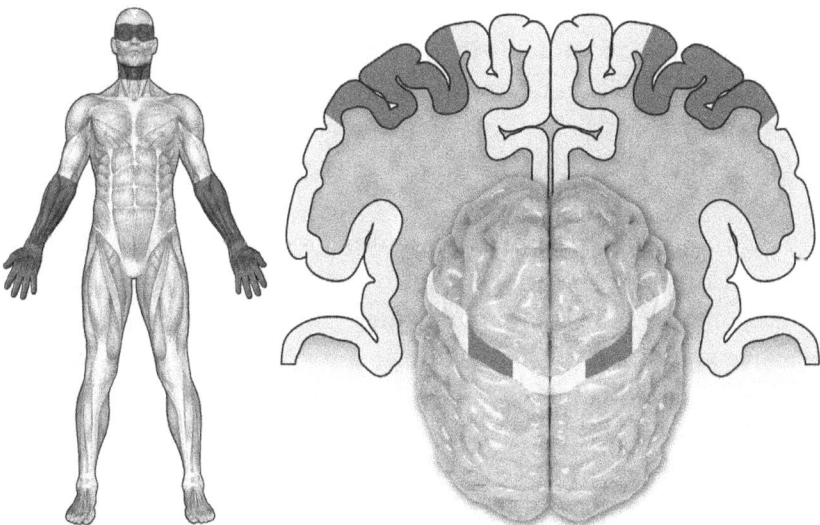

cortex, the next body skills the brain is naturally learning to expertly utilize are the fine motors—the arms, hands, and fingers. Again, every mother can attest to this. As the toddler begins to employ its arms, hands, and fingers more, virtually nothing is off limits to the young learning child, as it strives to grab, hang on to, and pick up things like never before.

Once again, it is very logical, based on the way the brain is constructed, that all people who are hardwired to Observe Impersonally are similarly genetically built to specialize in use of the fine motors. These Impersonal Observers generally have the ability to develop top-level hand-eye coordination. Star athletes of this design have included the likes of tennis' **Andre Agassi** (known for his devastating topspin forehand), baseball's **Alex Rodriguez**, and football's **Peyton Manning**.

Each and every Impersonal Observer is fine-motor dominant. Give them a baseball or bat, a football, a tennis racket, a hammer, or even a pencil, and you can detect their hand-eye dominance—especially if they have worked to develop it.

III. Face Region

While the initial stages of a baby's development come quickly and starkly, the next phase is more subtle and takes longer to evolve. Physically, the child begins to speak, specifically expressing itself with language. This entails heightened development of the jaw muscles, tongue, and lips, which engage the upper respiratory tract. Though these may not be commonly thought of as important "muscles" when considering physical growth, speech production and singing would not be possible without these crucial facial muscles. Sure enough, as we travel down the motor cortex, these very same muscles are found next.

As the human brain matures during this same time period of physical development, it is capable of making more complex links and connections to life. Some of these areas cannot be grasped by our five senses and, thus, must be understood by conceptualization and imagination—our "*sixth*" sense." These cognitive abilities begin to switch on as we develop speech, and link words and thoughts together—somewhere in the vicinity of age two for most children. These abilities will continue to mature, even into the teen years.

Note that the first two main stages of mental development all refer to "surroundings," due to the fact they interact with their *observable* physical environment. The nuances that can be detected by the five senses are areas that can be grasped and understood by all. As we venture into the conceptual world, however, the term "surroundings" is less applicable. Ideas, imaginations, theory, and abstraction can come from anywhere—especially from the deep recesses of the mind. Concepts can be like the wind, not easily grasped or comprehended. With this in mind, "surroundings" will be jettisoned as we explore the vast expanse of the conceptual universe.

One more note from a physical standpoint: During this stage of growth, while the muscles of the mouth and face are being refined, another physical aspect is taking place. The child is learning to better coordinate and harmonize the gross and fine-motor movements, linking the two together.

Quarterback **Tom Brady**, golf legend **Tiger Woods**, and effervescent former Olympic gold medal gymnast **Mary Lou Retton** all fall into this hardwiring category—the Personal Imaginers. As athletes, they not only can be the most coordinated and graceful, like many great figure skaters have been, but because of their mouth region of expertise, they are normally quite articulate and can express themselves well. Their tongues and lips naturally work better and faster than most other designs.

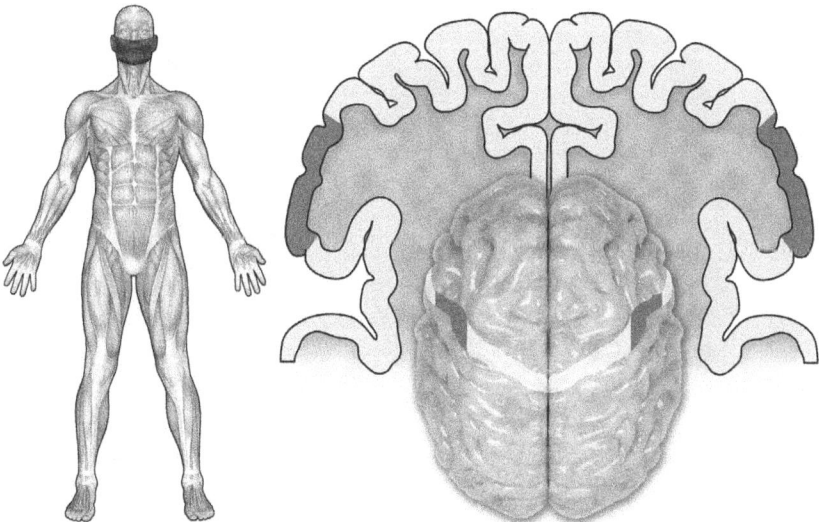

IV. Diaphragm Region

At this point, we have covered most of the significant muscles of the human body, but as we continue down the motor cortex, there is one more of importance. As with the prior muscle group, this final region also influences language and singing. Rather than the basic production of sound and speech, however, this area specializes in **voice** manipulation. What is the key to expert singing or voice manipulation? Many may not realize this, but the key to mastery of the voice is controlling the *flow of air*. It is a common misconception that the lungs optimally regulate air flow. For one thing, the lungs are not muscles, but rather internal *organs*. Because of this distinction, the major muscle controlled by the lowest region of the motor cortex serves an important function. It is principally the work of the thoracic diaphragm that makes the lungs function properly.

The thoracic diaphragm is shaped like an upside down bowl and is attached to the lower ribs. It separates the lungs and heart from the abdominal area. The diaphragm especially controls air intake, inhaling, and the release of air (not exhaling), regulating the voice, singing, even running. If you exhale quickly, your diaphragm is inactive. If you exhale very slowly, such as you would do when you are trying to feel a warm breath on your hand placed close to your mouth, the diaphragm is actively resisting the exhaling action of your abdominal muscles.

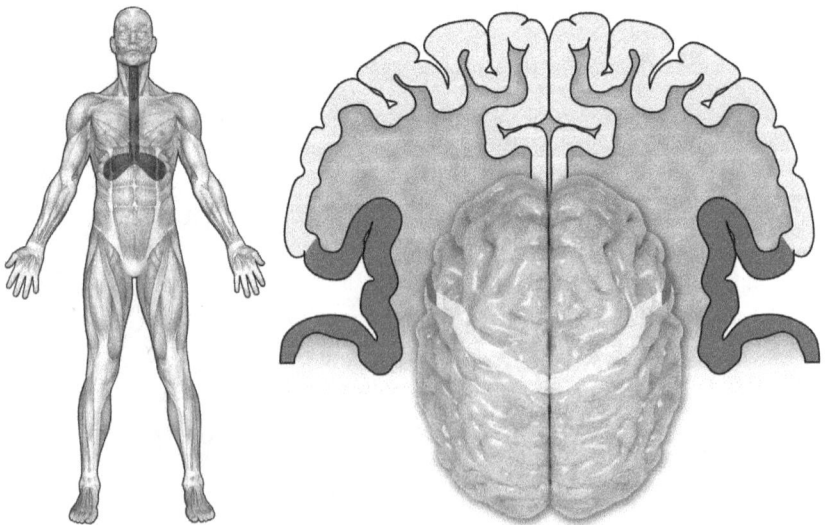

It is the diaphragm and some other internal muscles found in this lowest section of the motor cortex which are the final components to body development and expertise. These muscles regulate many functions not only necessary for voice manipulation, but used in strenuous athletics, as well—especially endurance sports like long-distance running. Thinking about a

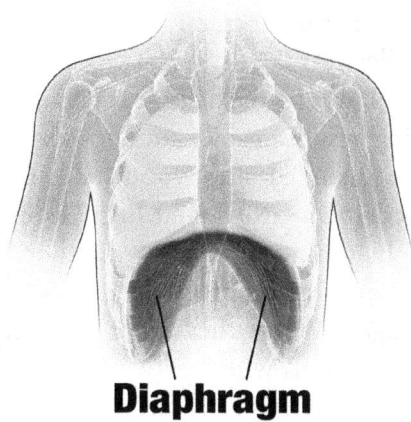

Diaphragm

child's physical development, once again, among the final areas in a typical child's growth is learning to manipulate air flow, normally manifested in the ability to produce a more melodious song.

Have you ever wondered what advantage the world's top singers, orators, and, especially, long-distance runners have over their competition? Even ventriloquists and "beat boxers" share this inborn hardwiring advantage. One vital component for all of their success is the ability to breathe properly—especially mastering air intake and optimal, controlled outward flow.

The diaphragm regulates the lungs, which are elastic and cannot function properly without the muscular diaphragm pushing the abdominal cavity lower, which, in turn, allows the lungs to expand and gather air. If you ever had the wind knocked out of you, it was your diaphragm that was rendered motionless, leaving your lungs with no mechanism to help them. Remember, releasing air or exhaling comes from essentially two sources, either as a result of the proper control of the diaphragm, or the abdominal, back, and other nearby muscles.

The final main stage of cerebral development coincides with this final physical period, and it shares a similar subtlety, as well. The growing child, who has already begun to refine its conceptual "sixth sense" now begins to turn its interest from *empathetic* thoughts of people and living entities to more *analytic* thoughts of matters in the inanimate world. Things and issues begin to take priority over people and emotions. This stage typically shows itself around age seven, though some born with the strongest hardwiring in this dimension can sometimes begin to display evidence of these traits as early as the toddler years!

Mastering the diaphragm, as the Impersonal Imaginers are best at doing, results in voice and breathing excellence! Impersonal Imaginers have included such vocalists as **Celine Dion, Barbra Streisand, Luciano Pavarotti**, and **Josh Groban**.

In summary, each of the four body skill groupings fully relies upon its brain to process cognition—such as in perceiving and giving thought. Where they differ dramatically, however, is in the various brain regions where each is most adept. In other words, each body skill grouping is cerebral and engages the brain heavily; they just rely upon different regions than one another.

3

The Four Cerebral Functions

In the previous chapter, we discussed the two basic mental functions—PERCEPTION and THOUGHT, as well as the pair of methods (observe/imagine, personally/impersonally) for engaging each. Now, we take a closer look in order to comprehend what is transpiring from a brain-related perspective. As we do this, some new terms will be introduced to illustrate how the latest scientific advances support the hardwired operation in each of the 16 unique inborn designs. These terms are also intended to make the revelation of hardwired designs easy to learn and comprehend.

As previously cautioned, when giving consideration to yourself and how you may be innately designed, it is important to be mindful that people rarely see themselves according to their true inborn nature. It is easy to be fooled by the effects of one's nurturing, especially when considering these insights for the first time. The terminology introduced here is intended to be more descriptive and accurate in order to reflect what is actually taking place within the mind. These terms are also less stereotypical of many conventional personality analysis terms. You will see how this is so as I point out some of the more familiar Myers-Briggs terms, from which this methodology arose, along with why those cause many conventional MBTI test-takers to fool themselves.

How One Perceives the Outside World
SENSING – "S"
CONCEPTUAL – "C"

These indicate which senses you naturally use first—the traditional five senses to OBSERVE (sight, hearing, smell, taste, touch) or the "sixth" sense—your IMAGINATION (intuition). Do you find yourself more drawn to what is actually observable and measurable, or are you fascinated by the possibilities in a situation? Are you more interested in *what is* or *what could be*? Do you find yourself focused on the "here-and-now," or does your mind wander off into daydreams? Virtually everyone does both to some degree, and nobody is all one way or the other. We all access each dimension. However, just as we each have two hands but tend to naturally favor one over the other, we are also each hardwired in such a way that we innately incorporate one way of perceiving the world over the other in the majority of situations. The best way to consider this is to try to think of how you or somebody you know is *more often than not.*

You will learn more about this after we have introduced the four quadrants of the brain and explain how this has a direct impact both on how you perceive matters and how you make decisions. Until then, focus on the general description of the terms for all four of these cerebral functions.

The Sensate (**S**) lives in the real world of the present. Sensates are pragmatic and enjoy impressions from their environment taken in through the five senses. They are observant and factual, most interested in the immediate usefulness of knowledge, while tending to shun the theoretical. One of the questions they continually ask is, "Will it work?" Sensates go through life trusting the tangible, the observable. They pay attention to detail and follow directions step by step. Direct conversation is their style, generally saying what they mean and interpreting what they hear and read literally.

Conceptual (**C**) represents the reliance upon one's own insights into the world of possibilities, concepts, significance, and absorbing information. It is the ability and tendency to easily imagine and visualize. The Conceptual enjoys symbols, daydreaming, and mental exercises that focus on the future. For the Conceptual, the here and now takes second place to the past and future. Facts are useful only to develop patterns that lead to further discoveries or that support thoughts and ideas already held. The driving force inside the Conceptual is to invent and create. **C**s are more apt to "read into things" and "read between the lines." The Conceptual who is permitted and encouraged to develop this giftedness is the dealer in ideas—the inventor, the novel writer, the research scientist, the journalist, the movie director.

In contrast to popular psychological type theory, our research has found that Conceptuals approximate well over half of the U.S. population—far more than commonly believed by conventional "personality" analysis. These Conceptuals (especially those who are Back-brain dominant, which you will learn about in the next chapter) often feel out of step in school until they reach college. Collegiate education tends to be more Conceptual-oriented and often finds the see-it-to-believe-it Sensates struggling to keep up.

The difference between **S**s and **C**s is wide and varied. Therefore it would follow that they need great tolerance of one another. Sensates may see Conceptuals as flighty, impractical, and out of touch with reality. To Conceptuals, Sensates may be viewed as short-sighted, nit-picking and unimaginative. Using one function or the other exclusively can lead one astray. We need the input of both functions—facts with possibilities, and dreams in touch with reality.

KEY CHARACTERISTICS	
Sensate (S)	**Conceptual (C)**
• informed by the five senses	• informed by "sixth sense"
• found in the present	• found in the future
• "Will it work?"	• "Is it possible?"
• perspiration driven	• inspiration driven
• motivated by usefulness	• motivated by inventiveness
• evidence seeking	• potential seeking
• the way it is	• the way it could be
• yesterday and today	• tomorrow and beyond
• directions	• hunches
• literal	• figurative
• tangible	• intangible
• observant	• imaginative
• pragmatic	• visionary
• inspired by the real, the practical	• inspired by the imaginative, the ingenious

How One Processes Information
EMPATHETIC – "E"
ANALYTIC – "A"

As discussed previously, after perceiving something, we process this information in one of two ways—either PERSONALLY or IMPERSONALLY. Decisions inevitably must be made, and people find themselves naturally making them based on either a more subjective, *personal* basis—their Empathetic (**E**) function, or on a logic-driven, *impersonal* basis—their Analytic (**A**) function.

One person may choose an impersonal, objective approach that seems to be clear and logical, while another may be prone to "feel a situation out," preferring to decide based upon more personal, subjective values. The latter usually places more emphasis on how the decision will affect the people involved, while the former is primarily concerned with the principle of the decision.

In fact, conventional typological theory associates the term "feeler" with Empathetic and "thinker" with Analytic. Of course, Analytic "thinkers" definitely have feelings and Empathetic "feelers" certainly do think. We know this because all brains possess both of these functions in their neural networks. As previously explained, however, each person is born with an internal circuitry that drives us to be naturally more proficient with one function over the other. This explains why people often do not "speak the same language." Those of us with a dominant Empathetic function possess what could be described as a high degree of *emotional intelligence*. Dominance in the Analytic function, meanwhile, results in a high degree of logical precision. In a situation affecting both Analytics and Empathy, these areas of specialty in decision-making often clash. We can have a major point of contention between opposing designs.

For example, consider two parents, each dominant in one of these two opposing functions. The Analytic parent may deem it appropriate to discipline a child by grounding the youngster immediately for poor behavior. Thus, the parent is "thinking" logically (Analytically). The Empathetic parent may consider such a penalty too drastic if it interferes with a social engagement the child had been looking forward to. In terms of relationships, that parent is also "thinking" rationally, but from a more "feeling" (Empathetic) standpoint. Conflict between the two perspectives is inevitable.

Both the **A** and **E** functions are rational processes, and both are necessary. In dealing with objective issues, numbers, and principles, we need the logical Analytic thought process. When dealing with people and animals (living creatures), the Empathetic process is generally more desirable. Unfortunately, many of life's dilemmas involve both realms, which necessitates wisdom in properly combining the two.

Empathetic-oriented people tend to make judgments or decisions more subjectively, placing extra emphasis on personal values. They consider the personal impact of a decision, causing them to be more personally invested in decision-making. They naturally gravitate to friendly persuasion over barked commands in order to make their point. Softer, friendly expressions and ready smiles provide telltale clues to their dominant **E** function.

To Analytics, their Empathetic counterparts may sometimes appear wishy-washy, unable to come to or stand by a firm decision that is tough on people. Empathetic **E**s show their thoughts in body language and may often be seen as emotional, illogical, or too "soft." It may be more difficult for them to express the logic behind their viewpoints. As a result, **E**s may need to consciously focus greater attention to the logical side of personal issues. If the values of **E**s are solid and true, however, they will often be just as "on target" as their logic-based counterparts, especially when it comes to decisions involving people.

Es are sympathetic to the emotional pain of others and show special sensitivity to those in need. They are more interested in people than things, preferring tactfulness over directness in most situations. Empathetics flourish with appreciation and general "good vibrations." Recalling past encounters and reminiscing are also **E** characteristics.

It should not be surprising that many women (probably taking into account society's prevailing "emotional" stereotype) tend to see themselves as Empathetics even when they are not. Analytic females may often find it beneficial to soften their image whenever possible. For most women, motherhood and cultural female behavior bring an extra measure of personableness. Even today, society often looks kindly upon a "warm-natured" woman.

Analytics are more apt to make decisions based on logical,

impersonal reasoning. They tend to be objective and rational, carefully considering rules and policy. They can more easily remove themselves personally from the decision (especially if they are dominant in the brain's left hemisphere, which is discussed in the next chapter). From the **E** perspective, the **A** may sometimes seem distant and hard-hearted.

Analytics seek objective truth, looking at situations in "black and white," using terms like "true" and "false," and "right" and "wrong." They use emotions and values only to validate logical conclusions. Analytics must be careful to ensure their deductions are based on valid data. To avoid hurting a friend, a wise **A** will learn at an early age to be tactful when telling the truth.

As you might expect, most men in our society (once again, due to cultural influence) refer to themselves as the equivalent of Analytics in many conventional "personality" inventories, probably because they see this description as more acceptably masculine. *Incidentally, there appears to be no material difference in the ratio of Analytics to Empathetics between men and women.* Among both genders, it appears that Analytics make up over 60 percent of the people in the United States. Remember, all people use both the **A** and **E** cerebral functions, but in every person, one is wired to be innately stronger. This is especially apparent when experiencing pressure (or stress).

Few people are at the extreme ends of the spectrum of **A** and **E**—from a persona perspective. Most people realize the importance of showing a balance to others, especially in social settings. Yet there are four designs (as you will learn) that are dominant Empathetics and four that are dominant Analytics due to their genetic makeup. These designs have to work the hardest in showing a balance of the two. Of course, their brains will always be stronger in their dominant function, but with persistence and focus, they can achieve a reasonable balance.

Consider this example that might be seen in a morning walk taken by two neighbors. The first person (**E**) is there to talk, to relate, to build the friendship, and secondarily to exercise. The second person (**A**) is out primarily for increased metabolism and exercise, while relationship and conversation are merely pleasant by-products of getting the workout in. If the **E** can't keep up the pace, the **A** may be moved to exercise alone.

We may see the difference in the example of a couple deciding how to spend a free evening. The **E** wants to have friends over while the **A** would prefer to spend the time working on a hobby. The **E** is drawn toward relationships, the **A** toward projects. It should be pointed out that Analytics often have a strong affinity toward their own family members and close friends, while Empathetics tend to broaden their scope of relationships.

KEY CHARACTERISTICS	
EMPATHETIC (E)	ANALYTIC (A)
• subjective	• objective
• interpersonal	• impersonal
• merciful	• just
• circumstantial	• lawful
• appreciative	• critical
• value-driven	• principled
• relational	• systematic
• caring	• cool
• persuasive	• commanding
• concerned with effects on people	• concerned primarily with issues involved
• personal reasons	• logical reasons
• concerned with emotional aspects	• unconcerned w/emotional aspects
• sympathetic managers	• firm managers
• tactful	• direct

4 x 4 = 16

You have now been introduced to the four most basic hardwired groups, which correspond with the most fundamental foundations of our hardwired designs—the motor skills connection. Next, we will introduce the final pair of dichotomies that make up our inborn circuitry—the cerebral locales—giving us 16 unique hardwired designs. With additional direct links to motor skills, as well as energy levels, comprehending Front vs. Back-brain dominance and Left vs. Right-brain dominance will take your knowledge of human understanding to another level. You will then be ready to really hone in on the specifics of each of the sixteen innate hardwired designs.

4

Cerebral Locales

The Four Quadrants

In addition to the four cerebral functions of our inborn designs we have discussed so far, there are four specific regions of the brain where the processing of information takes place. These final pieces to the hardwired design are what we will examine in this chapter.

The brain has two lobes, located side by side. These left and right hemispheres are connected by millions of nerve fibers called the *corpus callosum*, which acts as a "power transformer," regulating activity between the two hemispheres. In addition, each hemisphere has a front and back region—anterior and posterior. This combination results in four distinct quadrants of the brain. Each person in the world is innately strongest in one of these quadrants.

Neuroscience has revealed much about the workings of these regions of the brain in recent years. It was the detailed study of these findings, combined with the original work of Carl Jung and his later disciples that enabled Jonathan Niednagel to discover the underlying innate designs in people. By connecting the dots unveiled by modern science, Niednagel found a far more stable foundation and scientific basis for understanding human behavior than anything offered by conventional personality inventories. In particular, the neuroscientific findings regarding the left and right hemispheres were particularly revealing with regard to the body skill and spatial awareness aspects.

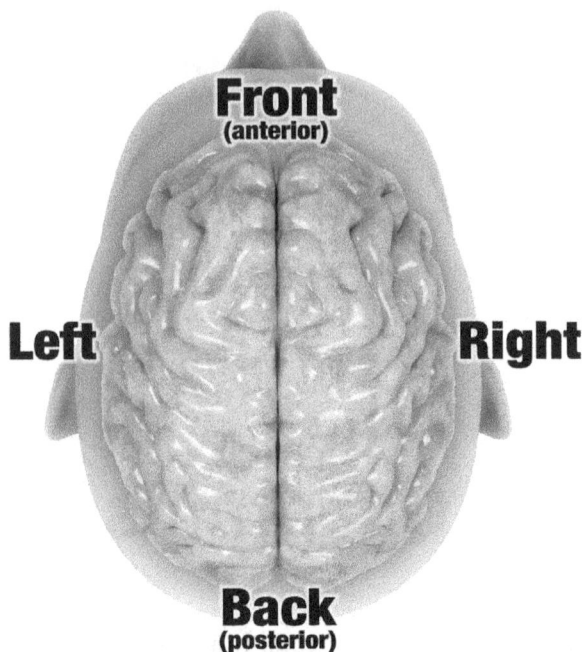

Front / Back

Every person is innately wired to be strongest in either the anterior part of the brain (Front-brain dominant – "**F**") or in the posterior (Back-brain dominant – "**B**"). Originally associated with the terms "extravert" and "introvert" as first applied by Jung, these may be two of the most misunderstood words in our vocabulary. When we hear the terms "extravert" and "introvert," we think of stereotypes—usually negative ones. Introverts have come to be considered self-absorbed loners who don't like people and don't like to go out in public. Extraverts, on the other hand, are considered "people-persons" who like to talk and enjoy being around other people—all the time!

If we discard any preconceived notions and replace them with the terms' original meanings, coined by Jung, we can see that he was attempting to identify *how people are energized* (how people get their energy). By understanding inborn hardwired designs, we can not only answer Jung's question, but we can now employ the latest advances in neuroscience to go further and actually identify the cerebral locale in which each person is most proficient.

Brain Processing ("introversion" vs. "extraversion")

Neuroscience research has revealed much about where in the brain specific processes occur. As knowledge from the external world is absorbed via the five senses (sight, smell, hearing, touch, and taste), these inputs are processed by the **Back** of each hemisphere. The Back of the brain focuses and *reflects* (Jung's "*introversion*") upon these inputs as it combines them with prior stored knowledge and translates them into meaning.

The **Front** of each hemisphere then *acts* (Jung's "*extraversion*") on these reflections or external needs, as it considers external circumstances. At the very front of the brain, just behind the forehead, is the prefrontal cortex, which is the most significant area for creating each person's outward "personality." Damage to this region can cause flattened inflection in speech, resulting in a subdued personality. It follows that people hardwired to be strongest in the Front of the brain are generally more verbose and speak with a louder, more varied tone.

The Front region is the "take-charge" part of the brain. In very general terms, Front-brainers (**F**) usually prefer to focus on the outer world and are energized by their contact with it. Their batteries are normally charged by talking and interacting with people, with activities, with living out their plans and dreams. Our research has revealed that nearly 80 percent of the United States population is hardwired in the Front brain—thanks both to early immigration factors and probable genetic dominance.

Front-brainers normally look for stimuli outside of themselves and have a wider scope of activities and interests. They usually say what they think or feel. They live life outwardly to gain inner understanding and generally need to be with others, but, as active people, they still need time alone in order to avoid becoming rundown. (It is important to keep in mind that many other nature/nurture/physiological factors can also impact social, persona, and energy levels to various degrees.) Confident Front-brainers can greatly enjoy time in the inner world, but their talents are best used in relating to others.

Front-brainers are consistently more energetic than Back-brainers, provided their brains are in healthy condition. This is often reflected with a quicker response time when asked questions. They tend to have better eye contact during conversation—especially when they are speaking, and are more open and direct in their body language. Many clues—verbal, as well as physical—distinguish Front-brain dominant people from their Back-brained counterparts.

Back-brainers (**B**), in contrast, are compelled to charge their batteries from within. Many Back-brain dominant people are inclined to keep their real selves hidden until they fully trust a confidant or until they know others will take the time to hear them out. Back-brainers build their energy when they have time and space to be alone. They are less distracted by activities around them, as they possess better concentrating abilities. **B**s generally conserve energy and delve deeply into interests and relationships. They have fewer acquaintances, since they tend to become drained by too much interaction. Through practice, or by being raised in an "extraverted" Front-brain dominant family, a Back-brainer may develop a good facility for Front-brained "extraversion." Remember, environment or upbringing can have a profound influence on one's persona. It will not, however, result in any change to a person's Front or Back-brain genetic configuration. What it can do is make an impact upon our natural predilections and inhibitions, as well as the personality traits of extraversion and introversion.

Back-brained Empathetics (**BE**s) may seem more Front-brained, for example, because of the natural development of relational and people skills. Operating in the Front of the brain is something they will continually seek in order to relate to other people. In a family setting or when with close friends, Back-brainers may be loud, outgoing, vivacious and seemingly Front-brain dominant. Their Back-brain preference for "introversion" will be seen more clearly, however, when they are in unfamiliar situations. Conversely, Front-brainers can appear like Back-brained "introverts" when, for example, they lack self-confidence or concern for others, and when they have been heavily exposed to a quiet or solitary environment.

As with all of the hardwired dichotomies, there are varying degrees of Front-brain and Back-brain proficiency. People who display extreme dominance in the Front-brain (normally the result of unique genetic or dietary factors) will be absorbed in action, crowds, business, rushing from place to place, and speaking extemporaneously. They would rather "do" than "wait." Back-brainers with extreme tendencies will be reclusive, painfully shy and retiring. Most people, of course, fall somewhere in between. Though atypical behavior may sometimes mask a person's true hardwiring, it normally takes just a little probing before answers start to surface.

We can all use our Front brain or Back brain at any time, but each of us will always be more prone to using one locale more than the other. That will normally be the region where we are specifically pre-programmed to be most adept.

KEY CHARACTERISTICS	
FRONT-BRAIN DOMINANT (F)	BACK-BRAIN DOMINANT (B)
• outer world	• inner world
• active	• reflective
• energy-expending	• energy-conserving
• aggressive	• reserved
• many acquaintances	• a few close friends
• intrigued by surroundings	• more concerned with self
• inspired by public activities, in midst of others	• inspired by private, solitary activities
• responsive before reasoning	• responsive after reasoning
• public	• private
• congregate	• meditate
• reasons out loud	• needs time to express
• conversational	• passive conversationalist with strangers

Left / Right

Next, we have the two hemispheres of the brain. Since the discovery of two brain hemispheres many years ago, man has had many questions regarding this strange anatomical quirk. Why would humans need two similar yet distinct cerebral lobes?

Neuroscientists have discovered that the **Left** specializes in concentrating on *one issue* at a time whereas the **Right** focuses on *many issues* at once. Both hemispheres process Back-brained "introversion," and Front-brained "extraversion," as well as the Sensing, Conceptual, Empathetic, and Analytic functions. However, each hemisphere handles these processes differently from the other. The Left brain processes information in an orderly, structured, deliberate fashion, while the Right brain does so in a more holistic, synthetic, flexible manner.

Conventional typology describes Myers-Briggs' "judging" as deliberate, seeking closure, and other terms highly compatible with the left brain and "perceiving" as adaptable, spontaneous, and other terms harmonious with the right brain.

Dr. Walter Lowen, State University of New York at Binghamton professor emeritus, first suggested the "judging" left brain, "perceiving" right brain association. The postulations in his book, *Dichotomies of the Mind*, provided instrumental support to Niednagel's findings. Dr. Lowen also suggested a direct link to motor skill activity. Subsequent brain mapping data added convincing supportive evidence.

Neuroscientific research has revealed much about how the two hemispheres function, which can be summarized in this table:

KEY CHARACTERISTICS OF THE TWO BRAIN HEMISPHERES

LEFT BRAIN	RIGHT BRAIN
• speech-skilled	• pattern-skilled
• exact solution	• sufficient solution
• sequential processing	• parallel processing
• orderly	• synthetic
• resistant to interruptions	• welcoming of interruptions
• skilled at reading, writing	• skilled at drawing, sculpting
• abstract categorizing	• understanding metaphor
• verbal, numerical logic	• spatial, visual logic
• generally positive	• generally moody
• work-oriented	• play-oriented

L vs. R

In determining whether someone is Left-brain dominant (**L**) or Right-brained (**R**), do not put too much emphasis on how they behave at work. Vocational arenas demand certain behaviors regardless of our innate tendencies. Think about the total person—how we naturally operate during everyday life.

Left-brainers are driven to take action and come to a decision or conclusion more readily. They desire closure in their outer world. Left-brained persons tend to be organized and decisive, and value advanced planning. They are geared toward making decisions about what they—and others—should do. They prefer to plan, maintain order, and to control events and people around them. **L**s do better with deadlines and living by the rules. Being more work-oriented, they want to get their work done before they play, believing that play must be "earned."

Wired strongest in the Left brain—the more emotionally stable hemisphere, they are essentially optimistic and cheerful, even amid difficult times. That optimism, however, may not always be readily observable, as they continually strive to put life in order.

Right-brainers generally require additional time dealing with the outer world before making decisions. They feel the need to continually gather additional information and make more observations, keeping their schedules and viewpoints fairly open-ended. This leaves them in position to experience the new and exciting, both for the Front-brainer and the Back-brainer (on the Right side). If you want to do something on the spur of the moment, call the spontaneous **R** person.

The Right brain is more emotional, negative and pessimistic than the Left brain. Right-brain dominant individuals are more flexible and adaptable. They shun the attempts of others to put them in a box. They avoid confinement and desire greater freedom with little or no restraints. If taken to the extreme, **R** persons may stray off course and lose control of their outer lives. **R**s need a degree of Left-brain function so that they can be aware of their boundaries.

Rs tend to receive new information in a non-judgmental, open-minded way, whereas **L**s are inclined to hesitate if new information fails to conform to preconceived knowledge. Years of research has revealed that well over half of the United States population is innately

Right-brain dominant.

In general terms, Left-brain dominance refers to someone who is innately conclusive and decisive—someone who is uncomfortable until decisions are made. Right-brainers are considered to be aware, absorbing information without experiencing pressure to arrive at closure. Both are rational ways of living, though one is more planned and the other more spontaneous.

KEY CHARACTERISTICS	
Left-brain dominant (L)	**Right-brain dominant (R)**
• organized	• flexible
• decisive	• exploratory
• "let's finalize"	• "let's wait"
• closed	• open
• work-oriented	• play-oriented
• planned	• adaptable
• control-loving	• freedom-loving
• deliberate	• spontaneous
• driven to decide	• driven to understand
• enjoys finishing	• enjoys beginning
• rigid	• wishy-washy
• avoids surprises	• welcomes surprises
• step-by-step	• hurry it up
• enjoys results	• enjoys the process
• "get to the point"	• "explore the tangents"

L vs. R Motor Skills

These Left brain and Right brain distinctions can be particularly visibly apparent in athletes. Their hemisphere dominance is clearly reflected in their actions and performance on the playing fields and courts. Meticulous observation of an **L** athlete reveals a more rigid, "mechanical" motion with less fluid movement. Because the left hemisphere is a sequential processor, the motor movements tend to be more deliberate. From swinging a golf club to throwing a ball, the **L** may even appear a bit "robotic," especially if relatively inexperienced. The **L** may have fine accuracy, but will normally appear less graceful when compared to an **R**.

Left-brainers tend to be more deliberate, almost "mechanical," in their movements. Naturally desiring quick conclusions, they act with purpose in a more "pre-determined" manner than their Right-brained counterparts, who demonstrate more grace, smoothness and spontaneity, naturally waiting as long as possible to make their moves. Though subtle, it can be quite apparent once you understand what to look for. Right-brainers, conversely, wait as long as possible to make their moves (continually open to new information), which tends to give them a more graceful, smooth, instinctive, and spontaneous athleticism.

For example, the **R** basketball player who dribbles into the lane and jumps will normally wait longer to decide to shoot or pass the ball than his **L** counterpart. In a sport like basketball, it is usually better to hold off making a decision until the last possible moment. This is one reason why **R**s make the best point guards. Rarely does an **L** point guard find success at the highest levels.

Think of the NBA's all-time best assist-makers and you will be thinking of Right-brainers. **Magic Johnson**, **John Stockton**, **Steve Nash**, **Jason Kidd**, **Oscar Robertson**, **Isiah Thomas**, and **Chris Paul** all share the trait of hardwired Right-brain dominance.

Even the occurrence of injury can be impacted by hemisphere dominance. Left-brainers are more inherently injury-prone due to their relative inflexibility. When balance has been lost or the body is otherwise susceptible to injury due to a particular body movement, **R**s have a tendency to fall (and roll) more gracefully, which, in those instances may result in fewer injuries. (Similar to how relaxed drunk drivers are sometimes miraculously preserved in auto accidents.) This is not to imply that **R**s are immune to injury, of course. In fact, even while naturally more limber, these open-minded, go-with-the-flow daredevils often encounter more than their share of bumps and bruises due to greater risk-taking than their more conservative Left-brained counterparts.

L vs. R Impact on Spatial Awareness (Vision)

Hemisphere dominance even influences our vision, or spatial awareness, which is especially apparent in the fast-moving world of sports. Left-brained athletes are cerebrally designed to see *one part* of the field of play in an *exact* fashion. While this can provide them with a detail-oriented view of their vision target, it also leads to "tunnel-vision" when experiencing pressure. This will cause the **L** quarterback to "lock" onto his intended receiver early or the **L** auto racer to not realize the car that has crept up next to him just as he is about to change lanes. Right-brainers, on the other hand, are designed to see the *entire field* of play in an *inexact* way. While they will not be nearly as detail-oriented in their visual perception, this provides them with greater peripheral awareness. They have a greater natural consciousness of everything taking place around them.

A vivid example of this is found in a story of how Bill Parcells, head coach of the New England Patriots, once helped a young quarterback overcome his **L** tendencies. Left-brainer Drew Bledsoe was the first player selected in the 1993 NFL draft. As the starting quarterback for the Patriots the following year, he led the NFL in passing yardage. However, he also led the league in interceptions, due to a troubling tendency to focus his sights on his intended receiver immediately after the snap, as he dropped back to pass. This allowed the defenders to easily discern where Bledsoe intended to throw the football, enabling them to position themselves, accordingly.

Parcells' solution was brilliant. As the story goes, he broke the field into thirds for his young QB: left, middle, and right. On certain plays, the direction Bledsoe looked as he dropped back to pass would actually be scripted into the design of the play. For instance, on a play designed to pass to the receiver on the right, Bledsoe was instructed to first look over the middle, then to the receiver on the left, before whirling to the right and finally picking up the teammate who was his primary target all along!

I have never been able to find published verification of this story, and I certainly doubt that coach Parcells realized he was dealing with a dominant Left-brainer. The issue being dealt with, however, was a classic Left-brained trait and the solution would be an excellent strategy for addressing the problem in a productive fashion.

Obviously, not all **L**s and **R**s perform alike. The impact of the other innate brain processes (F-B, S-C, E-A) are significant, with the various combinations greatly impacting performances of athletes who even operate from the same side of the brain.

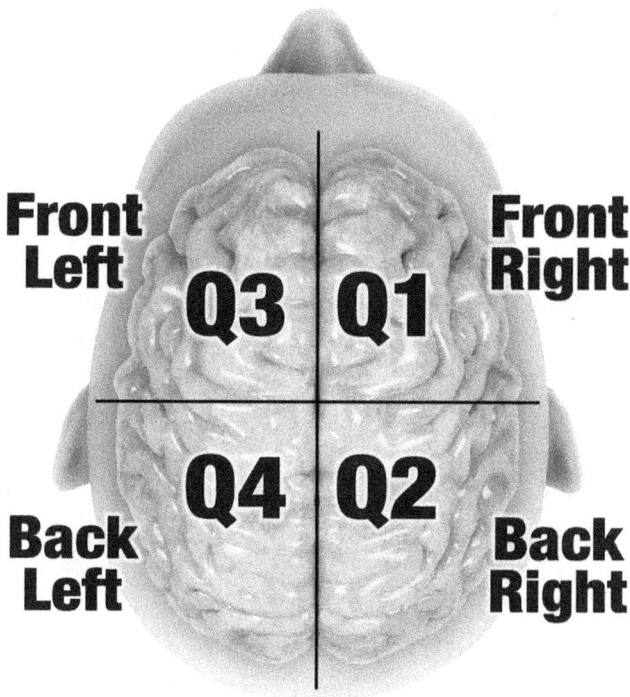

Front Left — Q3   Q1 — Front Right

Q4   Q2

Back Left — Back Right

The Four Quadrants

As we have introduced the four general locales of the brain (F & B, L & R), we will now take a closer look at the way combining these locales gives us four distinct quadrants. Similar to the motor cortex, these quadrants can be labeled in an orderly fashion, both due to the order of human development, which you will learn more about in chapter six, as well as their general order of function.

We begin with the most energetic quadrant, the Front Right, which we call Q1. From there, we transition to the posterior of the same hemisphere, the Back Right (Q2). We then cross over to the anterior region of the opposite hemisphere, into the Front Left (Q3), before moving finally to the Back Left (Q4). Each person is born strongest in one—and *only one*—of these four brain regions. Each quadrant specializes in specific mental traits, as well, which we will discuss next.

Cerebral Locations

We cannot pinpoint with complete certainty where all of the mental processes take place, due to the vast complexity of the human brain. We can, however, identify where certain processes demonstrate high activity levels.

It appears that each innate design excels in a particular region of the brain. While this does not limit access to other cerebral regions, each specific design is hardwired to be most neurologically efficient in a specific brain locale. It makes sense then that the opposite quadrant of the brain—the quadrant in the opposite end of the opposing hemisphere is where each design is least adept (i.e., someone wired to be strongest in Q1 is least adept in Q4, Q2 is least adept in Q3, etc.) This will be especially meaningful as we discuss the relationship to motor skills and how each design is prone to perform under pressure—both athletically and otherwise.

Q1 - Front Right (FR): *Explore (via S or C)*

We have already discussed how personality is a function of the Front brain—especially in the Front Right quadrant, which is known for its energy and enthusiasm. A strong personality is a good clue that you have a Front-brainer on your hands; a super-high or excessive personality leads you to the Front Right brain!

Intrigued by new and novel things, the FR quadrant (Q1) looks to "**Explore**," which it does either via the five senses (Sensing—*what is*) or through imagination (Conceptual—*what could be*). This first quadrant is interested in seeking (**S**) or imagining (**C**) something fresh or different. It can easily lose interest if it is not intrigued with its focus. This explains why the vast majority of children diagnosed as ADD possess a Front Right-brain (Q1) hardwired circuitry.

Any time we learn something new, Q1 tries to make sense of it first. This has been validated by brain imaging studies.

For athletes, the Front Right is especially accessed when the athlete is "in the zone" and Q1 Sensates engage it most easily in sports. This region also has superior vision—seeing what is and what can be—using both Sensing and Conceptual perception.

Essentially the fun part of the brain, Q1 is the risk-taking quadrant, driven by rewards, such as an adrenaline rush! The vast majority of thrill-seekers and the highest risk-takers are hardwired with Q1 proficiency. This includes athletes in sports involving risk with dramatic speeds or great heights, such as alpine downhill snow skiers, race car drivers, and "Extreme Games" competitors.

The Right prefrontal cortex can also excel in visualization and imagination; most movie producers, directors, and actors, as well as the majority of artists, and computer programmers are innately strongest here. Q1 has enormous drive, yet with adaptability and flexibility. Planning also occurs in the prefrontal cortex.

In addition, the Front Right quadrant is the most athletic region of the brain. Not only is it necessary for getting "in the zone," but it is crucial for fast-moving and fluid motor movements. The four designs strongest in Q1 are all top-notch athletic designs. Quadrant one is naturally superior athletically to the other quadrants.

Q2 - Back Right (BR): *Compare (via E or A)*

Moving to the posterior region of the same Right quadrant, we go to the Back Right. This Back Right (Q2) region is the home of internal feelings and logic. It is largely where Empathetic and Analytic thought functions are carried out. The deep limbic system, especially the right amygdala in men, is a primary emotional center. (The amygdala is an almond-shaped mass of gray matter found in each hemisphere.)

Spatial logic, which is heavily used in sports, drawings and paintings, or even to swat a fly, is largely manifested in Q2. Geometric shapes are of great interest to Q2—where Analytic Right-brainers excel. To excel at chess requires great mastery of Q2, utilizing its extraordinary spatial logic and memory.

This Back Right quadrant takes information—both new and old—and focuses on "**Comparing**" it with previous knowledge. Q2 carries this out via either a personal, subjective (Empathetic) or logical, objective (Analytic) thought process. Whether it be things, people, or even ideas, Q2 finds similarities or common characteristics, making connections. Note that these links may be both of the positive and negative variety. Q2 attempts to make some sort of connection even if the similarities are nebulous. When something new is learned, Q2 relates it to other things that have been learned in the past.

People wired strongest in Q2 may often need help in finishing major projects, as they are prone to easily get lost in thought. Though not naturally designed to be a CEO, by implementing self-disciplines, Q2 people can achieve much success.

Though the Left hemisphere is the home for most language skills, especially in men, both men and women use the Back Right brain to complement the Left. Q2 interprets nonverbal communication—such as facial expression, vocal tone and intonation, and other nuances of body language.

Q3 - Front Left (FL): *Critique (Contrast via E or A)*

We now transition over to the Left hemisphere, where we move back to the Frontal region, home of quad 3. This Front Left is most responsible for following through on things. Q3 complements its intense drive with controlled structure. Whereas Q1 might blurt out virtually anything that comes to mind, it is Q3 that stops us from putting our foot in our mouth. Expressing tact and discernment is possible only with a healthy Left prefrontal cortex.

It is not surprising that the world's zaniest comedians have dominant Q1 circuitry, while some of the best politicians are hardwired strongest in Q3! Right-brained politicians must make a conscious effort to give extra thought to what they say, as they will be more prone to utter an off-the-cuff remark in the spur of the moment. (U.S. President Barack Obama, who possesses a Q1 design, or his closest advisors must have unwittingly realized this fact, as his conspicuous reliance on teleprompters quickly became a staple of his public appearances.)

Like Back Right Q2, the Front Left brain also makes comparisons, but the interest is not in finding likeness, as in Q2. In Q3, the focus is "**Critique/Contrast**." Q3 determines how things are different, or *dissimilar*. Just as in Q2, Q3 carries this out with either a personal, subjective (Empathetic) or logical, objective (Analytic) thought process. Q2 and Q3 attempt to assist and balance each other in thought and decision making.

As an example, Q2 may consider the information in this book to be "similar to other personality information I have previously learned." When Q3 processes these insights, however, it will engage its critiquing and contrasting expertise, telling Q2 of all the ways hardwiring is vastly different and superior to other behavior/personality assessment methods.

The Front Left quadrant is known as the "executive control center" of the brain. Similar to an air traffic control center, Q3 directs signals from all parts of the brain, meticulously regulating various regions as it deems appropriate.

Exceptional at searching for and locating flaws, Q3 can be the most critical region, especially when expressing itself to others about differences. Ironically, Q3 can also be very positive. It is this Front Left quadrant which is responsible for tempering the emotional deep limbic system, protecting us from a constant state of depression. It loves to accomplish goals and pursue what it believes is right or best to do. Q3 says, "I see similarities, but allow me to point out the inconsistencies."

The Left prefrontal cortex is crucial for getting things done. As the brain's "CEO," Q3 enables us to finish projects, to bring closure. The four designs wired strongest in this region have the greatest natural self-discipline.

Q4 - Back Left (BL): *Classify (Categorize via S or C)*

Finally, we traverse to the final quadrant, Q4, located in the Back of the Left hemisphere. Wernicke's area is located here, which is heavily involved in the production of written and spoken language. Those suffering from dyslexia or who experience difficulty reading usually have some kind of problem with Q4 not functioning properly. It follows that the vast majority of people who have language problems are hardwired strongest in Q1—the furthest removed from Q4. Neural networks must be functioning properly in order to access this important language center.

Q4 is the most inquiring and scrutinizing of the four quadrants. This quadrant is where we file information, including people and ideas. Q4 specializes in "**Classifying**" and categorizing information, which it does with the five senses (Sensing—*what is*) or via the "sixth sense" (Conceptual—*what could be*). Q4 will not accept new information as fact or truth simply on its own merit. People wired strongest in this region are naturally skeptical of new information, whether it be ideas or people. Q4 prefers to dig deep in order to ensure it is properly categorizing any new information it comes across.

This Back Left quadrant finds a category or classification for everything that exists, or even claims to exist. Q4 considers its neighboring quadrants in order to make its decision about where something should be placed or slotted. It looks for similarities (Q2), but is more focused on the differences, which, of course, is the specialty of its closest neighbor, Front Left Q3. None of the other quadrants feel compelled to do this as does Q4—especially Front Right Q1, which may struggle to make the long, deep-thinking trek to the farthest away Back Left Q4. However, this can vary depending upon the health of the brain's neurons, as well as one's character and attitude.

The Left posterior (Q4) also helps us to modulate emotion and temper, to even control anger. (Q2 is the highly emotional and anger locale, especially in men.) Numerous brain studies reveal that criminals typically have dysfunctional Q4s. When Q4 is failing to function optimally—in any of us—we are less likely to implement precise language, emotional stability, or harmonious social behavior.

Long-term memory is stored on both sides of the Back brain. Spatial memory is heavily stored in the Right posterior (Q2), while language or numerical memory is principally in the Left posterior (Q4).

It is important to keep in mind that those hardwired to be strongest in Q1 (Front Right) are naturally second strongest in Q2 (the neighboring region of the same quadrant) and least adept in Q4 (Back Left)—the quadrant furthest removed. This works in reverse, as well, with those hardwired to be strongest in Q4 being next best in Q3 and least adept in Q1. The same goes for the relative proficiencies of Q2 and Q3.

Quad Specialists

To summarize, each of the four quadrants specializes in specific mental traits. Q1 and Q4 are specialists with the perceptive functions, Sensing and Conceptual. Q2 and Q3 are specialists with the thought functions, Empathetic and Analytic.

Q1 specializes in *exploring*, via what is (Sensing) or what could be (Conceptual). Q4 *classifies* in the same way by categorizing with either Sensing or Conceptual perception.

The specialty of Q2 is *comparing* via Empathetic or Analytic thought. Quad 2 is complimented by Q3, which *critiques* and contrasts with one of the same two thought functions.

You will learn more about this in the next chapter, as we close in on understanding how each innate design is specifically hardwired to function.

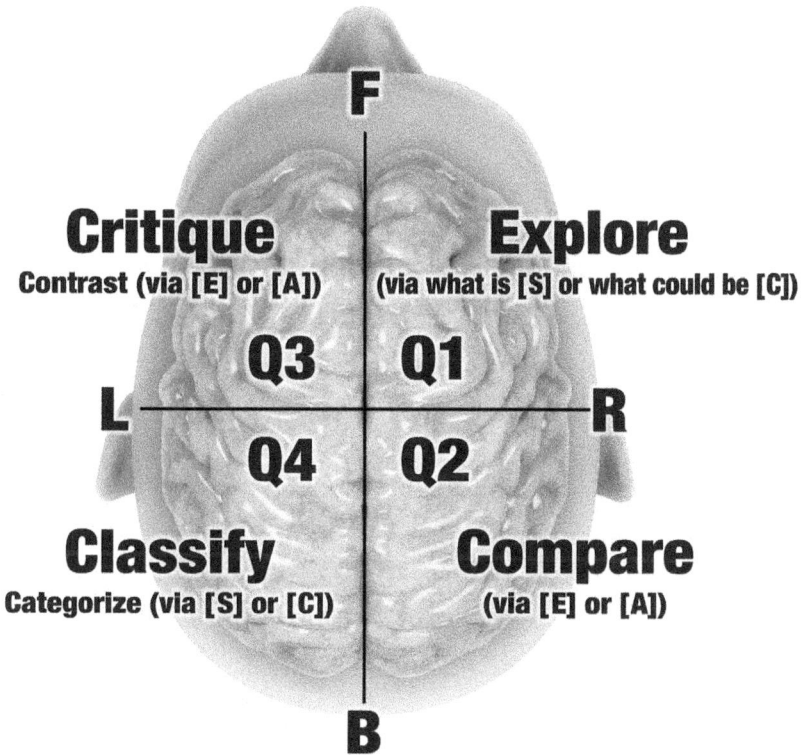

Foundation Set

You may be forgiven if you are feeling a bit overwhelmed by all of the technical information discussed in this chapter. While it may not be practical to digest fully in your initial pass, the latest findings in neuroscience provide crucial information for the foundation that explains what is taking place as we discuss each individual design in the second half of the book.

It is advisable to avoid getting bogged down as you read through this material for the first time. The best strategy may be to periodically return to this and other chapters throughout the first section for reference as you continue to gain comprehension of the way each person is specifically hardwired.

5

Orderly
Structure

One thing that should be quite apparent by this point is the orderly structure of our innate hardwired designs. It is in a beautifully systematic manner that the series of designs proceed down the motor cortex and similarly transition through the four quadrants of the brain. This remarkable *order* not only resembles an incredibly intelligent design, but also lends itself to a numbering system that helps with both understanding and remembering inborn hardwired circuitry.

The information contained in this chapter is helpful for understanding certain points that may be brought up in discussing the individual designs in subsequent chapters. However, it is important to not get hung up on some of the more complex aspects of hardwiring presented here. These ideas will gain clarity with time as you become more proficient in your comprehension of the sixteen unique indelible designs.

We begin at the base of the primary motor cortex, which we identify as region I, located just inside each lobe and circling over the top of the respective hemispheres. Here we find the gross-motor muscles, which are directly associated with Empathetic Sensates (Personal Observers). Proceeding around the quadrants of the brain from Q1 to Q4 as explained in the previous chapter, we have the first four hardwired designs as follows:

I-1   FRES: Front Right (Q1)
I-2   BRES: Back Right (Q2)
I-3   FLES: Front Left (Q3)
I-4   BLES: Back Left (Q4)

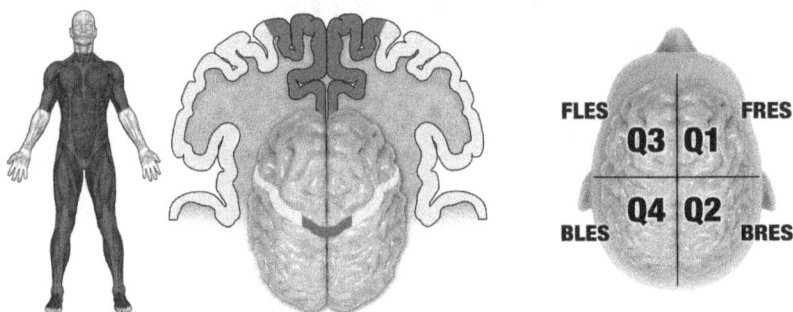

Next, we transition from the top of each hemisphere, down the motor cortex through region II, home of the fine-motors, associated with the Analytic Sensates:

II-1   FRAS: Front Right (Q1)
II-2   BRAS: Back Right (Q2)
II-3   FLAS: Front Left (Q3)
II-4   BLAS: Back Left (Q4)

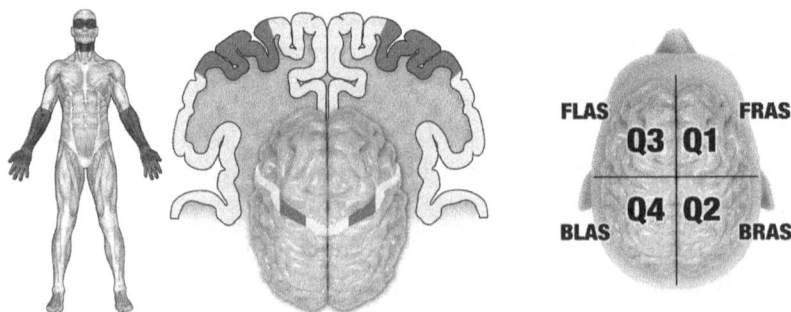

Continuing down the motor cortex, we find region III, which holds most of the facial muscles. We also transition from Sensing to Conceptual perception, starting with the Empathetic Conceptuals:

III-1 **FREC**: Front Right (Q1)
III-2 **BREC**: Back Right (Q2)
III-3 **FLEC**: Front Left (Q3)
III-4 **BLEC**: Back Left (Q4)

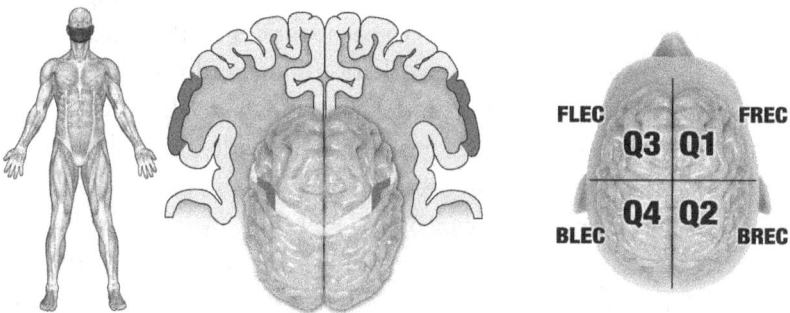

Finally, we reach the final section IV toward the bottom of the motor cortex. Here is where the diaphragm is found and where the Analytic Conceptuals reside. One more orderly trip around the four quadrants of the brain provides the final four numbers of our orderly hardwired numbering system:

IV-1 **FRAC**: Front Right (Q1)
IV-2 **BRAC**: Back Right (Q2)
IV-3 **FLAC**: Front Left (Q3)
IV-4 **BLAC**: Back Left (Q4)

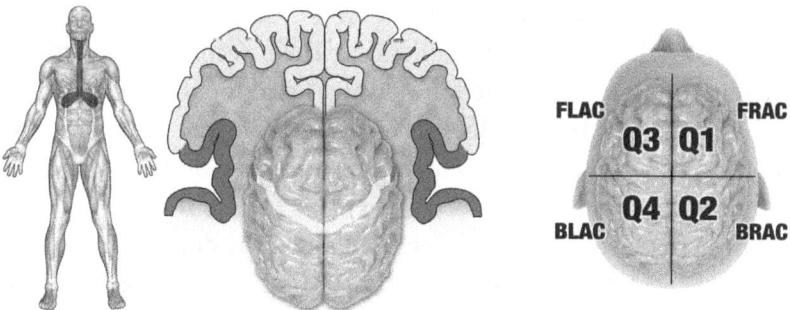

Function Dominance

As you know by now, each hardwired design is strongest in one perceptual function (Sensing or Conceptual) and one thought function (Empathetic or Analytic). Of these two mental functions, however, there is one with which each individual is innately most adept. This is referred to as the primary, or dominant function.

While it remains impossible at this point to fully understand precisely how the marvelous human brain performs all of the tasks it does, advances in modern science are constantly opening up new windows for us to gain clarity. These advances in the hard sciences provide the basis and the framework for understanding *what* the brain does, even if we still do not understand how or why it does those things. Innate hardwired designs finally provide an explanation of the brain's precise impact on personality, behavior, and performance. Function dominance is no exception. Here is how it works:

While the combination of mental functions for each design (I-ES, II-AS, III-EC, IV-AC) is directly correlated with the region of the motor cortex in which that design is most adept, the function with which each is most skilled has to do with the quadrant of the brain in which each specific design is wired to be most proficient. As we recall the manner in which each quadrant operates from the previous chapter, we can clearly see which function is dominant for each respective hardwired design. The other mental function of a given design—the one that does not appear in that design's quadrant—is the supplementary (supporting) function, meaning it is the one that ranks second in strength for that wiring.

For instance, Q1 designs are hardwired to Explore, using either their Sensing (what is) or Conceptual (what could be) function. Therefore, the I-1 FRES and the II-1 FRAS designs each have Sensing as their dominant function. Their secondary function is the remaining mental function—Empathetic for the I-1 FRES and Analytic for the II-1 FRAS. Their least proficient function is the opposite of their strongest, which, of course, is Conceptual for these two Sensing designs.

Either Sensing (S) or Conceptual (C) are the dominant functions for all of the *exploring* Q1 designs, according to their specific inborn

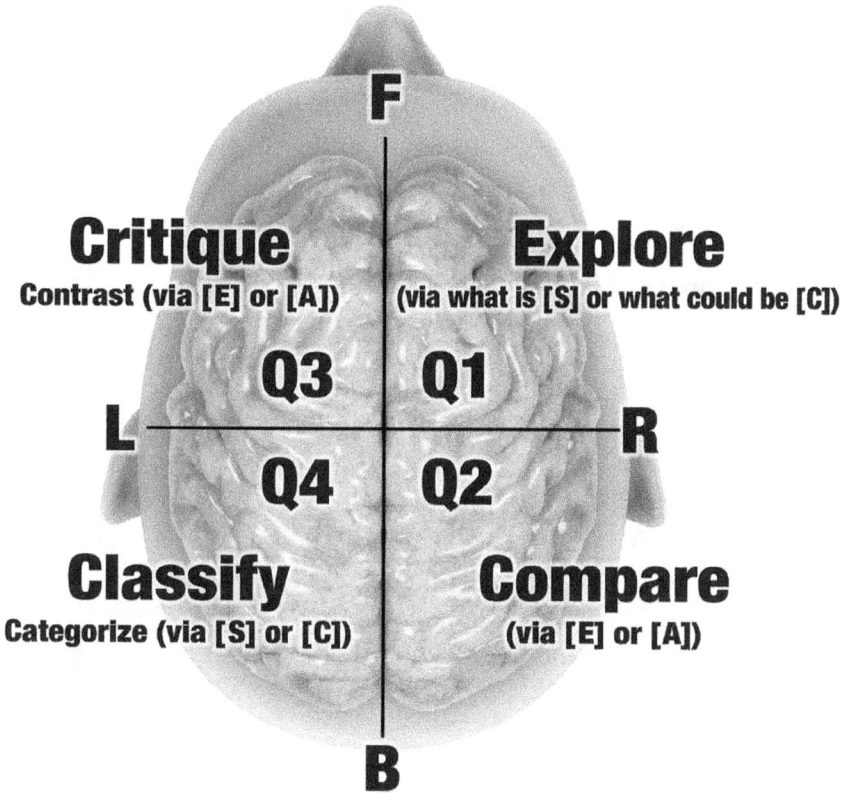

Critique
Contrast (via [E] or [A])

Explore
(via what is [S] or what could be [C])

Q3   **Q1**

L ——————————— **R**

Q4   **Q2**

Classify
Categorize (via [S] or [C])

Compare
(via [E] or [A])

F (top)   **B** (bottom)

neural circuitry. Moving back to Q2, remember that this quadrant is focused on *comparing* via A or E. It makes sense, then, that the designs found in Q2 (BR), have either Analytic or Empathetic as their primary function. Q3 circuitry specializes in *critiquing* and *contrasting* via A or E, so Q3 designs also have either Analytic or Empathetic primary functions. Finally, Q4 is the quad that is drawn to *classifying* and *categorizing* via S or C, which means that, just as with Q1 all of the Q4 designs are either primary Sensates or Conceptuals.

While the focus here is on where each design is strongest, it is important to remember that wherever a design is hardwired to be most proficient, the converse must logically represent where the innate circuitry has left it weakest.

ORDER OF FUNCTION DOMINANCE

Region I - ES

    I-1 FRES: Sensing, Empathetic, Analytic, Conceptual

    I-2 BRES: Empathetic, Sensing, Conceptual, Analytic

    I-3 FLES: Empathetic, Sensing, Conceptual, Analytic

    I-4 BLES: Sensing, Empathetic, Analytic, Conceptual

Region II - AS

    II-1 FRAS: Sensing, Analytic, Empathetic, Conceptual

    II-2 BRAS: Analytic, Sensing, Conceptual, Empathetic

    II-3 FLAS: Analytic, Sensing, Conceptual, Empathetic

    II-4 BLAS: Sensing, Analytic, Empathetic, Conceptual

Region III - EC

    III-1 FREC: Conceptual, Empathetic, Analytic, Sensing

    III-2 BREC: Empathetic, Conceptual, Sensing, Analytic

    III-3 FLEC: Empathetic, Conceptual, Sensing, Analytic

    III-4 BLEC: Conceptual, Empathetic, Analytic, Sensing

Region IV - AC

    IV-1 FRAC: Conceptual, Analytic, Empathetic, Sensing

    IV-2 BRAC: Analytic, Conceptual, Sensing, Empathetic

    IV-3 FLAC: Analytic, Conceptual, Sensing, Empathetic

    IV-4 BLAC: Conceptual, Analytic, Empathetic, Sensing

Outwardly Shared Function

There is an additional aspect of function dominance which is apparent only through understanding the intricacies of innate hard-wiring. As mentioned in the introduction, first impressions can be gained almost instantly upon meeting another person. To properly ascertain one's hardwired design, however, we must carefully consider additional aspects, even after making our initial read. This is because some designs do not naturally display their dominant function to others.

Take the energy-expending Front-brainers, for example. Naturally outward-looking and "extraverted," **F**s readily display their primary function to the external world. Their supplementary function is the one they use when they are looking inward, reflecting, more in the back of the brain. This is perfectly logical, as whatever quadrant in which a person is hardwired to be most proficient, the other quad of that same hemisphere is the one to which that design can most easily transition.

Looking at this simplified chart, we can see IV-1 FRACs, who reside in Q1, naturally show the world their exploring Conceptual function. When FRACs slow down and reflect, they readily move to the back of the brain in the same (Right) hemisphere to Q2, where they access their supplementary function—Analytic "thinking." Anyone in their presence when this reflection occurs will likely see a different perspective of their persona.

Now, here is where it gets a little tricky. All Back-brainers— regardless of hemisphere (R or L) dominance—need to "move" out of their (back quad) comfort zone and into their most accessible front quad (that of the same hemisphere) in order to readily interact with the external world. Because of this, Back-brainers may often be characterized by their *supplementary* function. Their primary function, meanwhile, is more readily utilized within their posterior introspective capacities.

Consider the II-4 BLAS design, for example. Hardwired strongest in Q4 (BL), this design specializes in critiquing via S or C. Since the BLAS is a Sensate (not a Conceptual), this design possesses a primary Sensing function. However, this primary dominance resides in the Back of the brain where the BLAS is most innately adept. The BLAS is more apt to show and deal with the external world using its supplementary Analytic function, found in the Front quadrant of the same hemisphere (Q3). This is neurologically essential, due to the fact that these external-dealing functions are found in the Front brain.

As a result, the II-4 BLAS may appear quite similar to II-3 FLAS

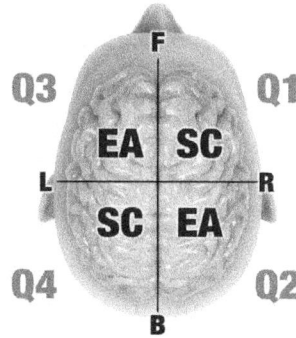

(Q3), which also displays to the world their Analytic function, due to the **A**'s inherent dominance in the FLAC's natural Front quadrant. Do not be fooled, however. Reaching quick decisions by the Analytic function is much more valued and readily implemented by the FLAS than the BLAS. Similarly, the BLAS prefers to gather Sensing data while *delaying* a final decision until after accumulating what is deemed to be sufficient evidence.

Again, it bears repeating that this material is greatly simplified to aid with proper understanding. As the tendency will be for those new to this revelation to consider each aspect of hardwired designs to be either/or propositions, this cannot be emphasized enough. Every person uses all functions, both outwardly and inwardly to various degrees. When experiencing "pressure" or "stress," however, in whatever form it may take, each individual relies on the strengths of his or her inherent hardwired design in terms of both behavior and performance.

In the area of self-understanding and improvement, comprehending the proficiency order of your mental functions will be beneficial. From an internal standpoint, it will enable you to more clearly identify and comprehend areas in which you must focus in order to gain "balance" in the way you operate. In regard to dealing with others, this knowledge can provide increased understanding and compassion.

Fundamental Mindset

By understanding function dominance, we can now take our understanding of each individual hardwired design to a deeper level. Considering the manner in which each design absorbs and processes information and combining that with the way each quadrant is hardwired to operate, we can isolate the fundamental mindset for each specific design.

First, remember that of the four basic functions, we have two representing Perception—*Observe (S)* and *Imagine (C)*—and two representing Thought—*Personally (E)* and *Impersonally (A)*. Then, recall the four quadrants of the brain and the specific way that each primarily operates. Q1 specializes in *exploring*, Q2 *compares*,

Q3 *critiques*, and Q4 *classifies*. More specifically, each quadrant carries out its operating mode in a particular manner.

Every design hardwired strongest in a particular quadrant is inherently designed to operate based on its innate neural circuitry.

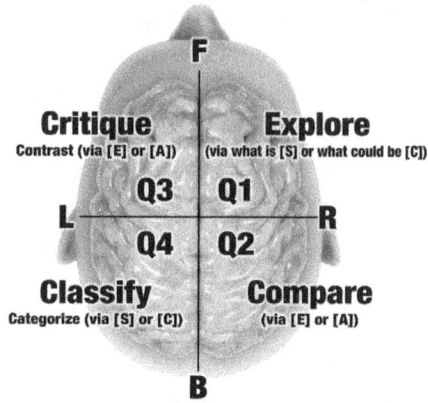

F

Critique
Contrast (via [E] or [A])

Explore
(via what is [S] or what could be [C])

Q3 | **Q1**

L ———————— **R**

Q4 | **Q2**

Classify
Categorize (via [S] or [C])

Compare
(via [E] or [A])

B

Q1: Explores via S or C

High-energy Q1, as would be expected, operates in brisk fashion, as it *quickly explores and responds to* its perceptions and thoughts:

I-1 **FRES:** Quickly explores and responds to observations personally

II-1 **FRAS:** Quickly explores and responds to observations impersonally

III-1 **FREC:** Quickly explores and responds to imaginations personally

IV-1 **FRAC:** Quickly explores and responds to imaginations impersonally

Q2: Compares via E or A

Located in the posterior, the Back-brained Q2 is, of course, more reflective and deep-thinking, as it *deeply compares and appraises* its thoughts and perceptions:

I-2 **BRES:** Deeply compares and appraises personal observations

II-2 **BRAS:** Deeply compares and appraises impersonal observations

III-2 **BREC:** Deeply compares and appraises personal imaginations

IV-2 **BRAC:** Deeply compares and appraises impersonal imaginations

Q3: Critiques/Contrasts via E or A

Returning to the Front brain, but in the more deliberate Left hemisphere, Q3 operates with more measured energy, as it *contrasts, acts on, and communicates* its thoughts and perceptions:

I-3 **FLES:** Contrasts, acts on, and communicates personal observations

II-3 **FLAS:** Contrasts, acts on, and communicates impersonal observations

III-3 **FLEC:** Contrasts, acts on, and communicates personal imaginations

IV-3 **FLAC:** Contrasts, acts on, and communicates impersonal imaginations

Q4: Classifies/Categorizes via S or C

The Back, Left quad is both deliberate and thoughtful, as it *methodically classifies and categorizes* its perceptions and thoughts:

I-4 BLES: Methodically categorizes observations personally

II-4 BLAS: Methodically categorizes observations impersonally

III-4 BLEC: Methodically categorizes imaginations personally

IV-4 BLAC: Methodically categorizes imaginations impersonally

In the next chapter, you will learn how every single person progresses through each of sixteen distinct mental *and* physical stages on the way to developing into an adult. We are each hardwired from conception, however, to be most adept in one and only one of these stages. As we reach this point in childhood, as well as after we have passed through all sixteen phases as adults, we remain specifically innately skilled in this particular area throughout our lifetime.

The way each unique design functions at its most fundamental level, as explained here, coincides precisely with the developmental stage in which each one is specifically skilled—not only mentally, but physically, as well. Every single person is hardwired with one specific design that corresponds directly with the same stage in the order of both physical and mental development each of us goes through and which that particular design is inherently most adept.

6

Piaget Explained

French psychologist Jean Piaget was the first to make a systematic study of cognitive development. Similar to Niednagel, and Jung before him, Piaget based his theory on the meticulous naturalistic observations of normal, ordinary people—in his case, children.

Piaget determined that children progress through four universal stages of development. While each individual child may progress through the stages at different rates, Piaget deduced that every child passes through each stage at some point and in the same order of progression.

Although Piaget made his determinations without the benefit of modern day advances in the hard sciences, the evident progression of hardwiring falls right in line with Piaget's theories of development.

Piaget's Stages of Development

Piaget identified four basic stages of human development. I will highlight them here with a brief description so that we can see how Piaget's discovery fits in neatly with the more detailed development illuminated by hardwiring.

1. Sensorimotor Stage (birth-2 years)

The thought process of an infant is, of course, extremely egocentric. Even as a young baby begins learning, all accumulated knowledge comes exclusively from the baby's perspective. Piaget felt the first key marker in cognitive development occurs when the toddler is able to form a mental representation of an object, thus knowing the object still exists, even if it is hidden from view.

An understanding of hardwiring reveals that this process is likely associated with Conceptual development, which generally begins around the end of the second year. In dominant Conceptuals, however, this ability may become evident sooner.

2. Preoperational Stage (2-7 years)

The second stage occurs in the range of two through seven years old. During this period, children develop the ability to think about things symbolically, making a word or an object stand for something other than itself. The child will still have difficulty focusing on more than one aspect of a situation at the same time, while thoughts and communications remain egocentric.

As you will see shortly, this second stage coincides with the initial Conceptual development of the four quadrants.

3. Concrete Operational Stage (7-11 years)

Piaget considered this third stage to be a major turning point in the child's cognitive development, as it marks the start of the ability to employ logic with operational thought. Thinking becomes more organized and rational, allowing the child to process information and solve problems internally, as opposed to physically working them out.

Interestingly, this stage appears to coincide precisely with the beginning of Analytic Conceptual development.

4. Formal Operational Stage (11+ years)

Beginning around age eleven and continuing into adulthood, Piaget's final stage is associated with developing the ability to think about abstract concepts, and logically test hypotheses. This, of course, would represent advanced Conceptual thought and coincides nicely with the final stages of human hardwiring development.

Developmental Attenuation

Consider the phenomenal development of a human from the point of conception to birth. Then, think about the rapid growth, both mentally and physically, of a newborn. Progress can be visibly measured in days initially, then weeks, and eventually months and years.

It makes sense that the developmental pace would naturally decrease. It also should be no surprise that the more complex development would take place during this extended late growth stage.

In the following pages, we will examine more closely the natural path of human development, along with the structure of the human brain and its accompanying hardwired circuitry. Especially for mothers, but also for anyone who has spent significant time around babies and young children, much of the imagery presented should be readily apparent.

For instance, what is the first thing a newborn does once it emerges into the world? It activates its five senses, of course, responding to each of them emotionally. Physically, the newborn first learns to utilize the big muscles, wiggling the body and moving its limbs, albeit in a rather haphazard manner. Mom may experience this gross-motor development even before childbirth as she feels the baby kick while still in the womb! It is no coincidence that all of these physical and mental functions are associated with the first region (section I) of the primary motor cortex, located at the top, nearest the center of the brain.

People hardwired to be most proficient in this region are blessed with gross-motor fluidity, outstanding spatial awareness, and superior emotional intelligence throughout their lives. In fact, we can see clearly how the natural development of every person flows along a structured path down the motor cortex and around the four quadrants of the brain. While every person passes through each one of these sixteen distinct stages of development on the way to adulthood, we are each specifically hardwired to be most proficient in the skills associated with one specific stage. This proficiency potential is denoted by the brief "giftedness" description that accompanies each stage of development on the following pages.

Intelligent Development

The orderly path of human development begins, just as would be expected, in the first region of the motor cortex, at its base, nearest the center of the brain. Development proceeds in a systematic manner from quadrant one through quadrant four before transitioning to the next region of the motor cortex and beginning, once again, at Q1.

Region I, Quad 1 (I-1 FRES) - "Social Performer"
Senses surroundings and responds Emotionally
GROWTH STAGE: Newborn
MENTAL: Immediately following birth, the baby begins to quickly incorporate use of its five senses, responding to them *emotionally*. The baby extraverts, using the Front brain—especially Q1—in order to get attention and express wants/needs.
PHYSICAL: Newborn flails its limbs as it makes use of the big muscles for virtually all movement at this early stage.
GIFTEDNESS: Incomparable spatial awareness with the capacity to master all five senses, in addition to gross-motor fluidity. High emotional intelligence.

Region I, Quad 2 (I-2 BRES) - "Harmonious Free Spirit"
Emotionally interprets Sensing surroundings
GROWTH STAGE: Days and weeks immediately following birth
MENTAL: The emotional interpretation of the five senses is taken to another level as the still very young baby gains the ability to *emotionally interpret* its surroundings, such as discerning that it enjoys being held in Mom's arms. It may not yet understand how to communicate this thought, but the mind has developed the capacity to process what is being experienced.
PHYSICAL: Motor movements are similar to that of stage I-1 in that they remain basically gross-motor oriented, though the infant begins to gain a degree of control in these movements.
GIFTEDNESS: Extraordinary emotional intelligence with an ability to have a special rapport with others and a desire for harmony with its surroundings. Just as with stage I-1, this stage has the ability to become a superior athlete, with super smooth moves.

Region I, Quad 3 (I-3 FLES) - "Personable Provider"

Emotionally expresses Sensing surroundings

GROWTH STAGE: 4-6 months

MENTAL: Though the baby has not yet learned how to speak, it is gaining the ability to *critique* what its five senses encounter and express how it feels, accordingly. As this stage involves the brain's communication center (Q3), the baby begins to find other ways to communicate, including mimicking its parents or other things in its environment.

PHYSICAL: It is always a big day in the baby's development when it finally learns to roll over. It is during this stage that the infant is developing *control* of the big muscles, learning the basics of how it needs to move and place them to create the desired result.

GIFTEDNESS: High emotional intelligence with an inclination to take action based on learned values and judgments. One of the top communicators, with a strong desire to express themselves.

Region I, Quad 4 (I-4 BLES) - "Guardian"

Classifies and categorizes Sensing surroundings Emotionally

GROWTH STAGE: 6-12 months

MENTAL: As the development of the young baby completes its first extended trip around the four quadrants of the brain, it subconsciously begins to classify and categorize all of its experiences and the emotions associated with them. (i.e., hugs, tasty food, full tummy good; cold drafts, indigestion, dirty diaper bad.)

PHYSICAL: As the baby's development transitions from energetic (Front-brained) to tempered (Back-brained) gross-motor control, the baby learns to crawl and then soon after to pull itself up and begin walking across the floor—another big day in any baby's development!

GIFTEDNESS: As this stage learns how to properly categorize and store all of the emotions it identifies, those hardwired strongest in this region grow to become guardians of their body, their mind, and everything around them. Though low-key people, they are very conscientious and reliable.

Region II, Quad 1 (II-1 FRAS) - "Quarterback"

Senses surroundings and responds Logically

GROWTH STAGE: Moving into the second year

MENTAL: Though still relying greatly on the five senses, the toddler begins to examine and respond to circumstances differently, as it processes observations and sensations more objectively and thoughtfully. This is especially noticeable in the spatial/visual realm where the child utilizes depth perception and gains comprehension of angles. The child makes extensive use of sight at this stage excitedly exploring its environment with Q1 energy in a new, unemotional manner.

PHYSICAL: The child begins to use its hands with more precision, grabbing, picking up, and latching onto virtually anything it can reach, and then putting the object into its mouth or elsewhere, much to the parents' chagrin. This makes perfect sense as the child is developing its fine-motor positioning at this stage.

GIFTEDNESS: Tremendous spatial awareness complemented by the ability to respond with blazing fast Analytic reasoning. Outstanding "street smart" instincts, capable of pulling off shrewd business deals in quick fashion. With superb vision, spatial logic, and hand-eye coordination, athletes hardwired with this circuitry are particularly gifted for playing quarterback, point guard, and any other position where seeing the entire field of play and making split-second decisions is critical.

Region II, Quad 2 (II-2 BRAS) - "Intense Artisan"

Logically interprets Sensing surroundings

GROWTH STAGE: Continuing in year two

MENTAL: The child develops spatial thinking, as thoughts and opinions begin to be formulated with unemotional Analytic reasoning. Using the back of the brain (Q2) during this stage, the toddler gives more reflective thought to its Analytic processing.

PHYSICAL: Fine-motor positioning becomes more pronounced as the child increases its ability to recognize and understand angles, patterns, and features of its environment.

GIFTEDNESS: With a superior ability to discern precise angles and other aspects of its environment, this design is capable of developing a supreme sense of timing for recognizing and capitalizing on opportunity. Expert hand-eye coordination can be used for artistic drawing, as well as passing the ball with expert precision. Intense competitors, practicing their craft is more pleasure than work.

Region II, Quad 3 (II-3 FLAS) - "Director"
Logically expresses Sensing surroundings
GROWTH STAGE: 18-24 months
MENTAL: By this point, the toddler has a good idea of its likes and dislikes, and as it begins to speak words, the child strives to communicate its thoughts from an impersonal, Analytic perspective. Again activating the communication center of the brain (Q3), the child is driven to share with the world what it has noticed, experienced, and decided regarding its surroundings.
PHYSICAL: The fine-motor hand-eye coordination becomes increasingly noticeable as the child operates with increasing control and dexterity.
GIFTEDNESS: Driven to help others organize their surroundings. Capable of easily finding differences, contrasts, and flaws in its environment, and readily verbalizing these findings to others. A natural born supervisor and director.

Region II, Quad 4 (II-4 BLAS) - "Perfectionist Inspector"
Classifies Sensing surroundings Logically
GROWTH STAGE: Two years old
MENTAL: A human's initial development of its five senses generally occurs during the first two years of life. As we reach the end of that period, the child begins to categorize things, similar to stage I-4, but now does so by incorporating Analytic logic, rather than the emotional perspective used earlier.
PHYSICAL: Controlled fine-motor dexterity continues to develop as the child gives more thought to its use of the hands.
GIFTEDNESS: Great capacity for quantifying impersonal reality, with the ability to observe Analytic matters in its reflective, dominant Sensing mode. With a penchant for going deep into its areas of interest, people of this design can become experts in their field.

Conceptual Growth (Stage III & IV)

We now transition to the second half of mental development, which takes longer and involves what some describe as the "sixth sense" of abstraction and intuition. As the human brain matures, it is capable of making more complex links and connections to life. Some of these areas cannot be grasped by our five senses and must instead be comprehended by conceptualization and imagination. These cognitive abilities start to switch on as we develop speech, and link words and thoughts together. It will likely begin around the age of two for most children, though these abilities will continue to evolve into the teen years.

We have witnessed the most commonly considered motor skills to this point, as well. We will now see more specialized physical aspects develop during these more complex developmental stages.

While a general age range is listed for each of these stages, the actual timing may differ by individual, based on many variables, including both environmental and genetic factors. The important takeaway is the order of development, as both mental and physical continue to proceed in an orderly fashion down the motor cortex and around the four quadrants.

It is also here where Piaget's work can be readily identified. In particular, Piaget's first "Sensorimotor" stage, which he identified as occurring during the first two years of life, is likely associated with the initial development of region III, marking the beginning of Conceptual growth. Though the age range listed here is the third year of life, it would be expected that early signs, such as those identified by Piaget, could be discerned earlier, especially in dominant Conceptuals.

Piaget's second stage coincides with the remainder of region III Empathetic Conceptual growth. It would follow that only after the child learns to deal with his or her emotions Conceptually would come the ability to think from the viewpoint of others. This begins as the hardwiring evolution enters stage IV, around the age of seven, just as Piaget observed. Indeed, just as Piaget considered this to be a significant development in a child's cognitive development, stage IV represents the most complex stage of progress for hardwiring circuitry. Those born with giftedness in these stage IV regions may exhibit related proficiencies earlier, while for others it may come later.

Region III, Quad 1 (III-1 FREC) - "Motivational Dynamo"
Conceptualizes and responds Emotionally
GROWTH STAGE: Third year
MENTAL: The high-energy Right brain (Q1) is now engaged again and, as with prior Q1 stages of development, it is highly aware of its surroundings. For the first time, however, the brain is concerned with the more intangible—that which cannot be easily measured or observed with the five senses. Impressions and possibilities take precedence as fantasy and make-believe become part of the brain's processing. Leaving the world of reality is a giant leap and this stage serves as the launching pad for a whole new way of engaging with the world.
PHYSICAL: As the child begins to string words together and speak clearly in simple sentences, it should be no surprise that the facial muscles are the next area of physical development. Specifically, the jaw muscles, tongue, and lips, which engage the upper respiratory tract. In addition to this energetic speech fluidity, the child also begins to coordinate the big and small muscles it learned to utilize in stages I and II.
GIFTEDNESS: A high-energy motivator with superb emotional intelligence. Excels at inspiring people toward rewarding possibilities. Masters of not only fluid speech, but also athletic fluidity. Expertly coordinates the big and small muscles with Front-brained energy and Right-brained smoothness.

Region III, Quad 2 (III-2 BREC) - "Imaginative Romantic"
Emotionally interprets Concepts
GROWTH STAGE: Age 3-4
MENTAL: The Back brain is at work again, interpreting the abstract world of emotional vibrations it is receiving from its Conceptual environment. It loves harmonious combinations and is adept at creating them.
PHYSICAL: Development of the mouth region continues with more tempered speech fluidity as voice inflexion and intonation become paramount.
GIFTEDNESS: Top-notch emotional intelligence with natural attention to vocal tone—*how* something is said, as opposed to

simply what is said. This design may develop a keen interest and proficiency in language and poetry.

Region III, Quad 3 (III-3 FLEC) - "Enthusiastic Teacher"
Emotionally articulates Concepts
GROWTH STAGE: Age 4-5
MENTAL: We are now back to Q3, which houses Broca's area—the language center of the brain where speech originates. As the brain is now able to process intangible thoughts, more advanced speech can be realized. Words take on special meaning, as ideas and concepts are emotionally articulated. Children at this stage take pleasure in informing others and acting on accumulated abstract emotions and values.
PHYSICAL: We see the continuance of speech development through the mouth region of the face, but it is now more Left-brained speech control, with words more measured and precise.
GIFTEDNESS: Wonderful communicator, not only due to mastery of language, but also via the adept coordination of the mouth region. Possesses unmatched ability to be diplomatic, tactful, and encouraging.

Region III, Quad 4 (III-4 BLEC) - "Caring Counselor"
Classifies Conceptual surroundings Emotionally
GROWTH STAGE: Age 5-6
MENTAL: Once again in Q4, the most scrutinizing part of the brain, the child learns to categorize all of its Empathetic concepts and imaginations, engaging a new region of neural networks. The child learns that every word has a specific meaning, and strives to find the one appropriate for each situation.
PHYSICAL: The final stage of development for the muscles through the mouth and ear region of the face, the youth now exhibits more tempered speech control. This may be a very subtle continuation of the progress that has previously taken place in stage III, as more thoughtful activity is taking place in the Back-brain Q4 region. In fact, language skills via the spoken word may take a back seat to reading and writing.
GIFTEDNESS: With a special appreciation for words, especially

literary and enriched language that touches the heart and soul, people hardwired with this circuitry have an unmatched knack for saying the right things at the right time.

Region IV, Quad 1 (IV-1 FRAC) - "Creative Strategist"
Conceptualizes and responds Logically
GROWTH STAGE: Age 7-8
MENTAL: As Conceptual development continues, the child engages Q1 one more time, though things and issues take priority over people and emotions. This is when the growing child masters the ability to conceptualize, learning to weave issues together that have a common logical thread, and offering an intelligent, impersonal response. Q1 loves new things and has a propensity to get bored quite easily. While this stage is typically encountered around the age of seven, children hardwired with this circuitry may sometimes exhibit noticeable traits as early as the toddler years. These high-energy designs may also easily exhibit symptoms of ADD if they find themselves bored in the classroom or otherwise.
PHYSICAL: The final portion of the motor cortex influences speech and singing, but unlike stage III, which handles the mouth region, this section specializes in voice *manipulation*. It is the thoracic diaphragm, which makes the lungs function properly by regulating air flow. In this stage, the child learns mastery of energetic voice fluidity, holding a note in song and controlling air flow for any purpose, including intense (opera-style) singing, serious acting, and athletics.
GIFTEDNESS: This multi-dimensional design loves to solve problems (and may even be found creating problems to solve when none seemingly exist!). With proper incentive, they will find a way to accomplish virtually any task, including becoming a high-level athlete. Though not naturally blessed with gross or fine-motor proficiency as some other designs, the FRAC can develop excellent skills with practice and proper training, strategizing with their fertile mind to find a way to achieve success in their chosen sport or field.

Region IV, Quad 2 (IV-2 BRAC) - "Einstein"
Logically interprets Concepts
GROWTH STAGE: Age 10+

MENTAL: As Analytic Conceptualization moves to the Back-brain region of Q2, the child begins to develop abstract spatial thinking, forming opinions and theoretical logic via Analytic reasoning. As much of the mind's time during this stage engages the thoughtful Q2, the child may exhibit more periods of introversion.

PHYSICAL: Development and use of the diaphragm that originated in Q1 continues, though much more tempered as this growth stage is devoted more to deep Analytical thought.

GIFTEDNESS: An innate drive to delve deep into and make sense of matters and issues with Conceptual complexity. This design has the ability to discern logical patterns in a maze of obscurity and abstraction.

Region IV, Quad 3 (IV-3 FLAC) - "Charismatic Leader"
Logically articulates Concepts
GROWTH STAGE: Age 10+

MENTAL: Once again in Q3, the most verbose and take-charge region of the brain, the child really begins to logically articulate concepts. Incisive thinking and hair-splitting logic is cherished in the verbal form, as meaningful ideas and concepts are articulated in a sound, sequential, highly rational fashion.

PHYSICAL: Voice manipulation here features more Left-brained control—helpful in speech-related activities, as opposed to the Right-brained fluidity developed in Q1 and Q2.

GIFTEDNESS: Master debaters, blessed with a high energy level, those hardwired with this circuitry are born leaders with an innate C.E.O. mindset.

Region IV, Quad 4 (IV-4 BLAC) - "Original Engineer"
Categorizes Concepts Logically
GROWTH STAGE: Age 10+

MENTAL: As we reach Q4 with the last motor cortex region, we come to the final basic stage of human development. This meticulous and analytical cerebral region is the engineering and inventor stage of the brain's development. Here the child learns to take the most abstract thoughts and make something useful from them. More than simply ideas, this stage seeks to produce something new and productive from what it discerns.

PHYSICAL: The final development of voice control. Because of their mastery of the diaphragm, all of the stage IV designs (the versatile Q1 FRAC, especially) can learn to speak with little lip and jaw restriction, becoming top-notch vocalists, actors, orators, ventriloquists, and "beat boxers." They comprise most of the top long-distance runners, as well.

GIFTEDNESS: Categorizing concepts logically with numerous files, diagrams, and writings of ideas in its brain. This design is then compelled to build a tangible structure by which to support these thoughts. Complex problems and projects require the design, development, production, and operation of competent and workable systems. Those hardwired with this circuitry are ideally suited to engineer an original solution, accordingly.

Summary

Each person is blessed with a unique genetic design from conception. While we all proceed through every developmental stage during our formative years, each of us is innately hardwired to be gifted in the skills associated with one—and *only* one—of these sixteen specific stages. While we may develop relative proficiencies in multiple stages, especially those closely related to our specialty, no one is expertly proficient in all stages.

In fact, we are inherently weakest in the area that is the exact opposite of our individual hardwired design. A stage IV-I FRAC, for example, is weakest where its complement, the I-4 BLES is strongest. That is, classifying and categorizing Sensing surroundings emotionally is the weakest process for the FRAC, which specializes in conceptualizing and responding logically.

Part II

THE
HARDWIRED
DESIGNS

7

Proper Design Identification

The natural inclination when learning something such as the material in this book is to wonder, "What design am I? How is she hardwired? What about him?" As you considered the information in Part I, it would be surprising if your thoughts did not turn to yourself, your spouse, your children, your extended family, your coworkers, your boss, well-known celebrities, and more! However, please heed this warning that your initial instincts may well be wrong.

As continually emphasized throughout the introduction of this information, none of the aspects of hardwired designs occur in a vacuum. Every facet exists on a continuum in relation to its pair, and in conjunction with the other factors, all of which combine to form the basis of each person's unique makeup. The remainder of this book will focus on helping to sort out the clues that can lead to the proper identification and understanding of one's inborn hardwired design.

Comprehension of hardwired designs can be fulfilling. It can be liberating. It can even be instrumental in dealing with those around you more effectively. In fact, consider virtually any aspect of life involving people, and it is difficult to fathom a realm where understanding hardwired designs is not beneficial. It is helpful not only in knowing the innate circuitry that is with you for your entire life, but it can also help you to *live life to the fullest!*

Know Thyself

We all size up people virtually every day. The key is doing it properly. The knowledge of hardwiring provides us—for the first time—the objective means to do so in a meaningful fashion. Of course, before we undertake discerning others, it is imperative that we understand ourselves. In fact, *"know thyself"* is perhaps the most famous of the ancient Greek maxims carved into the Temple of Apollo at Delphi. Classical Greek philosopher Plato writes of its usage by his mentor Socrates on multiple occasions. In short, the meaning is that exploring knowledge of other things (and people) is pointless until one has gained substantive understanding of oneself.

It may come as a surprise that numerous studies have demonstrated the way we view ourselves quite often differs greatly from how others see us. It follows, therefore, that the view we have of ourselves may, in fact, be quite different from how we truly are. In essence, our *nurture* may cloud the inborn *nature* of our innate design.

Whether due to the manner in which we were raised or because of other values acquired along the way, we many times view ourselves—and try to train ourselves—in the way that we wish to be or, at least, *believe* we should be. The result is often detached from reality, sometimes greatly so. Giving honest consideration to the information presented in this book, in addition to getting the honest perspective of others who know you well, can be very beneficial in gaining a true measure of self-understanding. Once we have substantive and objective knowledge of our own perspectives, we can then begin to rationally examine those of others in our lives. After conducting a thorough self-analysis, you may already see others in a new light, considering that they may not be wired in a similar fashion. Then, again, you may be enlightened to similarities with people you once thought to be quite different, yet now find to possess a similar design. You will see more clearly how this might be so as you explore the different designs.

I grew up thinking that I was very different from my little sister. Of course, there *were* differences. I was a boy and she was a girl. I enjoyed sports and, thus gravitated toward developing my motor skills, while she turned to interests of her own. Imagine the revelation years later to learn that she and I, in fact, share a similar basic inborn circuitry! Naturally, there are differences even within that same design—no two people are *exactly* alike—but looking back to the time of our youth, I now understand why we butted heads at times. It was not because we were so *different*. It was because we were too much *the same!* We are both very competitive, though that trait manifests itself differently within each of us, and we don't take "losing" easily. The result was that I viewed her as the "annoying little sister" at times while she probably viewed me as the "domineering big brother." While I have always loved my sister, I can honestly say that understanding our respective inborn designs gives me a much better appreciation for her today than I ever had growing up.

Sherlock Holmes

Because none of the aspects of our innate circuitry are "black and white"—we are not all "one way or the other"—making a proper assessment entails an almost never-ending search for clues. Even people of similar basic designs may very well have subtle differences that can be misleading on the surface. Further investigation, however, will reveal the true underlying design. The insights of hardwiring reveal a depth of person that goes far beneath the surface layer of personality.

Unfortunately, today's "smart phone" instant-information society has fostered a natural inclination for many who first become exposed to hardwired designs to get the idea that they can easily identify the inborn circuitry of others. One may be inclined to quickly label someone who displays emotion to be an Empathetic "feeler" or somebody who doesn't say much a Back-brained "introvert." While these statements could well be accurate, they often are not. In becoming who we are today, a variety of factors are at work, not the least of which is the significant impact of nurture on one's outward persona. Even with people you believe you know quite well, it takes patience along with a trained and discerning eye to really piece together the many clues that can lead to an understanding of one's true inborn design.

With adequate study and careful attention given to various nuances in behavior, you will soon begin to discern even the designs of people you do not know so well. It is all a matter of keeping an unbiased mindset and combining all the clues you can uncover until you are able to piece together what seems to be one's probable hardwiring. Even after you settle on a design for yourself or somebody else, it is best to remain open to the possibility that you may be off the mark as evidence continues to emerge. Never forget that while there are indeed telltale observable patterns in every person, it is also true that people are frequently very complex! Over time, validation or contradiction of your initial assessment will become self-evident. You will also find that you are able to increase the speed at which you can discern certain aspects of one's hardwiring as you begin to notice similar traits in different people of the same design.

Best of all, you will find yourself becoming much more appreciative of others' perspective as you give increasing thought to the fact that every person you meet has a specific inborn neural circuitry. This innate hardwiring, which is also impacted by each person's environment, gives that person his or her unique outlook on the world and manner of dealing with it. By approaching every situation with that in mind, you will find that communication and understanding—two of the biggest obstacles we face in dealing with people—become much easier than ever before!

The Young Children Conundrum

Determining the innate design of young children can be especially problematic. Youngsters often may not be particularly conversant and they also have a tendency to interpret questions in an unconventional manner. Depending on their level of education and life experience, they may not fully understand a question, yet may be inclined to provide an answer regardless. This may lead to frequent misinterpretations of their true indelible design. The same investigative evaluation process applies, nevertheless.

Obviously, assessing your own children should be easiest, as you have the inherent advantage of accumulating numerous clues in observing their daily behavior. However, this familiarity can also be a danger in correctly identifying their true hardwiring, as you may well have raised them in a certain manner, which has shaped their behavior to a large degree. For instance, a Front-brainer raised as an only child may be taught to quietly read, watch television, or play on the computer. This learned behavior can result in the appearance of a quiet, "introverted" Back-brainer to the casual observer. Similarly, a Back-brained energy conserver raised in a large family may learn to behave as an "extravert" when dinner is served, lest they hang back and go hungry.

I once worked with an Analytic IV-1 FRAC who frequently hugged people as part of his greeting. This behavior is common to many of the "feeling" Empathetic designs, which led many to conclude him to be hardwired, accordingly. Further investigation, however, revealed that he was raised by a (probably Empathetic) mother who loved to give hugs, both to him as a youngster, as well as others. Chalk up another case solved with "Sherlock Holmes" detective work!

Where to Begin

The best approach for accurately evaluating others—especially children—is by careful observation of their appearance (facial and dress), conversations, behavior, attitudes and motor movements. Listen in depth to the thoughts, syntax, diction, and voice inflection. This takes time, yet is vital for proper identification of one's true design. I will point out specific clues to look for as we get into each specific design, but I cannot emphasize enough the importance of continually gathering evidence as you are considering someone's inborn circuitry.

The following pages present some general signs that may serve as a good starting point for analysis. Keep in mind, however, that these aspects of a person's behavior are far from comprehensive and are not intended for thorough accuracy. As I have explained, not only are these characteristics found in combinations rather than singly, but each dyad is on a continuum that may make it more or less apparent in each person. They can be difficult to distinguish on a questionnaire, yet can be revealed much better through interactive interrogation, as well as careful observation. Therefore, remember to use the following indicators as merely a starting point in your investigation into discovering one's true hardwired design.

As you read the descriptions and traits attributed to certain designs throughout this book, keep in mind that such designations are referring to people who *possess* that design, of course. Also, you may find that the descriptions of design aspects sometimes switch back and forth between the singular and plural reference. This is simply a function of discussing traits of a particular design (singular), as well as that of people hardwired with such a design (plural).

Front-brain dominant
- High energy level, sociable, looking for places to expend energy
- Outgoing, like to "make things happen"
- Seek many tasks, public activities, interaction with others
- External, communicative, expressive
- Active, initiate

Children...
- High energy level ("loud"), look for opportunities to expend energy
- Always seem to be active (either physically or mentally)
- Talk more than listen
- Prone to "act," then "think"
- Think aloud (thoughts often "roll off tongue" without prompting)
- Naturally outgoing, enthusiastic

Back-brain dominant
- Reserved, soft-spoken
- Shy, do fewer things
- Seek more private, solitary activities with quiet to concentrate
- Internal, reticent, hold things in
- Reflective, deliberate

Children...
- Relatively low energy level ("quiet"), seek opportunities to conserve energy
- Listen more than talk
- Cautiously approach new situations
- Prone to "think," then "act"
- Think quietly in head (keep thoughts to self unless prompted)
- Self-contained, reserved

Note that overall energy level is a significant indicator of Front vs. Back-brain dominance, based on the neurological functioning of the brain. When considering "energy," take into account *mental* as well as *physical* energy. In fact, mental energy (provided medication is not part of the equation) can often be more demonstrative of a person's inborn hardwiring, since physical activity is not consistently encouraged in today's electronic gadget-crazed society.

Left-brain dominant
- Organized, orderly
- Thrive on having a schedule, an organized plan
- Regulated, structured
- Value preparation, work-minded
- Desire control, to govern
- Naturally pay close attention to time, schedule ("prompt")

Children...
- Single-minded, prefer to have matters regulated and organized
- Overtly judgmental and opinionated
- Maintain tidy, organized environment
- Serious, conventional
- Make decisions easily, desire structure
- Motor movements can be described as deliberate, mechanical, "robotic," with a subtle element of rigidity.

Right-brain dominant
- Flexible & adaptable, prefer to keep matters "open-ended"
- Tend to keep schedule relatively unplanned, spontaneous
- Easy going, "live and let live"
- Go-with-the-flow, play-minded
- Desire latitude, freedom
- Less aware of time ("always running late")

Children...
- Flexible in approach to dealing with matters
- Open-minded
- Difficulty keeping self tidy and organized
- Playful, unconventional
- Have difficulty reaching decisions, "go-with-the-flow"
- Motor movements can be described as fluid and smooth—even if relatively "uncoordinated," will appear more "loosey-goosey" or unrestricted than "mechanical"

Empathetic

- Compassionate, feeling, accommodating
- Tactful, kind, encouraging
- Gentle, tend to appreciate, conciliate
- Tenderhearted, merciful
- Sensitive, people-oriented, compassionate
- Draw conclusions more on basis of compassion and empathy

Children...

- Concerned with feelings of self and others
- Seek harmony, show compassion
- Act sad or hurt when criticized
- Motivated by appreciation, pleasing others
- Need and enjoy affection, affirmation
- Decisions heavily influenced by "feelings," (of self *and* others)
- Try to promote harmony whenever possible

Note that while they are greatly concerned with feelings of self and others, Empathetics are not always peacemakers.

Analytic

- Logical, thinking, questioning
- Candid, straight forward, frank
- Firm, tend to criticize, hold the line
- Tough minded, just
- Matter of fact, issue-oriented, principled
- Draw conclusions on basis of factual, unemotional logic

Children...

- Value fairness, rules, issues, "right" and "wrong"
- Ask "Why?" a lot
- Motivated by achievement, reaching goals
- Act somewhat uneasy with affection (both receiving *and* giving)
- Seek logical explanations, convinced by rational arguments
- Tend to sacrifice harmony with others to get point across

Sensing

- Interpret matters literally, rely on common sense
- Practical, realistic, experiential
- Standard, usual, conventional
- Consider immediate issues, focus on here-and-now
- Interested in the tangible; facts, things, seeing "what is"
- Prefer practical solutions

Children...

- Like to participate in action games
- Prefer nonfiction, reality, fact-based stories
- Notice details, focus on facts and specifics
- Gravitate toward toys that imitate real life
- Concerned with "fitting in"—e.g., fashion, what others are doing/wearing, etc.
- Notice details, remember facts and lists (see the "trees")
- Plain spoken, use ordinary language

Conceptual

- Look for meaning and possibilities, rely on foresight
- Imaginative, innovative, theoretical
- Different, novel, unique
- Look to future, global perspective, "big picture"
- Interested in the philosophical; ideas, dreams, ("what could be")
- Enjoy creative ideas

Children...

- Enjoy theoretical, strategic games of the mind
- Prefer fiction, imaginative, fantasy-type stories
- Notice possibilities and novel usages
- Focus on the "big picture"
- Vivid imagination
- Prefer unusual toys that stimulate creativity
- Enjoy being different—not preoccupied with social trends, etc.
- Focused more on the whole, ideas, concepts (see the "forest")
- Verbally precocious

Accuracy

The characteristics listed on the preceding pages can provide good indications, though they are far from foolproof. Here is why: If each person possessed only one dimension rather than a combination of all eight, he or she would be easy to figure out! Someone proficient only in Analytic "thinking" with no Empathetic "feeling" adeptness, for example, would be rather easy to assess. We must keep in mind, however—*and this is very important*—that everyone has a combination of each trait, and to varying degrees. Each person's unique mix affects the impact of the other traits.

Another issue is that quite often people do not take a very realistic view of themselves or their children. Though we tend to be more objective with regard to our spouse and others, it is important to gain an "outside" perspective when considering yourself or your children. One reason could be that we often view our children as an extension of ourselves. That is, we see what we believe to be aspects of ourselves in them, which may skew our interpretation of their true design.

For example, Analytic parents will generally not be as sensitive to their children's relationships with others as Empathetic parents. Also, Analytic Right-brainers will normally be more tolerant and easy to get along with than their Analytic Left-brained counterparts. The combination of Right-brain dominance with Analytic "thinking" can greatly lessen the impact of the **A** in an Analytic's personality. If an Analytic (either **L** or **R**) is taught to place value on people and treating others kindly, he or she can get along easily with others. As you can see, this may be used as an indicator, but is by no means infallible.

It is also important to keep in mind that diet, exercise, discipline and other life habits can contribute to one's appearance, especially children. The way a child eats has a very significant impact regarding the variations within each design. A child born with some dysfunctional neural genes or transmitters may be more adversely affected by poor nutritional habits. This may skew the appearance of their true hardwired design.

As I have tried to emphasize, if you continue to carefully search for clues the true innate design will eventually show itself. Do not forget, each and every person is born hardwired—*for life!*

Beware Corruption

Unfortunately, valuable information of any kind can be used destructively, regardless of how valid it is. There will always be those who misuse and pervert that which is inherently good. This must not stop those who would use beneficial information for constructive purposes. As you continue your journey to greater appreciation and understanding, the way you look at yourself and others will never be the same.

As you learn more specific characteristics of each unique hardwired design, keep in mind that these are merely generalized descriptions, which will closely fit the majority of people sharing that innate circuitry. There will always be exceptions, due to extraneous influences, such as environment, neurotransmitter health, etc., making some people a tougher "read" than others. Don't give up! Continue to thoughtfully investigate, observing carefully with an open mind. Clues will eventually reveal themselves in some form, leading to the identification of one's true indelible design.

8

How to Be
Like
Sherlock Holmes

By now, you have surely got the message loud and clear that properly uncovering one's hardwired design involves a continual investigation until enough clues add up to point toward a probable conclusion. However, even then, it is important to be on the watch for new clues to emerge. Even if the initial diagnosis is supported, new insights can be gained as to where on the proverbial design spectrum one is innately located.

In this chapter, we will discuss how to begin collecting clues and, in turn whittling down the possibilities. Always keep in mind that not all people within a particular hardwired design may fit the "typical" description so neatly. Upbringing (environment) has much to do with either the enhancement or suppression of one's innate traits, leading to a range of "personalities" within each design.

In order to narrow down the probabilities of what one's hardwired circuitry might be, it is often helpful to isolate the possibilities that can safely be ruled *out*. Also, try to avoid working through each pair of dimensions individually, one by one. It is usually beneficial—and necessary—to consider multiple aspects together. This is due to the fact that the brain quadrant in which a person is most dominant may result in several unique cognitive, as well as physical traits.

It is especially important to consider the whole person. While an individual may consider himself or herself to be wired in a certain manner with regard to one pair of dimensions, objective consideration of the whole person can often reveal otherwise. Though at first glance this may be perplexing, further thoughtful consideration will usually bring amazingly crystal clear illumination.

Though you will certainly begin by assessing people you know well, starting with *yourself*, the same basic process can be used with anyone, including even observing a stranger for the first time. That is what makes hardwiring superior to all other purported "personality" measurement methods. Because it involves examining self-evident outward traits of one's inborn neural circuitry, hardwired designs can be ascertained without the use of convoluted questionnaires or hit-and-miss Q & A sessions. Over time, you will become more adept at incorporating this process into evaluating others, so take your time and let the answers come to you.

Impressions First

One of the first things to notice is the subject's appearance. Flashy, colorful clothing and accessories provide strong clues of Front-brained circuitry. Back-brainers are more apt to be conservative and modest in appearance. Of course, this makes sense as Front-brainers are more naturally inclined to share their "personality," while their Back-brained counterparts are more apt to keep theirs hidden.

Sensates will tend to have more awareness of the current trends and styles, while Conceptuals may be more oblivious to, or at least less concerned with the latest in fashion. However, this general rule of thumb is complicated by the fact that Empathetics, who are innately aware of others, may also be in tune with fashion trends, due to the attention given to people.

Remember that these are all simply clues that serve to point us toward an accurate identification. Keep this in mind as you read the description of each individual design throughout the remainder of Part II. The combination of function dominance that makes up each hardwired design leaves an unmistakable footprint when enough evidence is pulled together.

Face the Truth

As explained earlier, the many muscles that make up a person's facial structure provide clues as to the underlying internal circuitry. Empathetics will tend to show a warm appearance, with a smile that is naturally evident. Front-brained **E**s, especially, may be apt to "wear their heart on their sleeve." Conceptual Analytics may tend to have a "head-in-the-clouds" look at times, as they are more caught up in their thoughts than the goings-on around them. Even hairstyles—and hairlines—can be evidence of specific hardwiring, as you will see.

Talk the Talk

Speech is another good indicator of innate hardwiring. It is important to listen in depth to the thoughts, syntax, diction, and voice inflection. This is especially true with children. Front-brainers will tend to be more verbally expressive while Back-brainers may be more naturally soft-spoken. Sensates will tend to talk more matter-of-factly and down-to-earth, while Conceptuals may be more ethereal in their vocabulary with a theoretical bent. Left-brainers will tend to be more deliberate while Right-brainers may have a tendency to ramble with less structure.

Sensates are more aware of their surroundings ("what is") while Conceptuals will be more focused on ideas and theory ("what could be"), which is often reflected in their talk. Similarly, Empathetics may be more talkative when it comes to topics involving people and living things, while Analytics may be more verbal when it comes to numbers and other material subjects.

Walk the Walk

Because the primary motor cortex is an inherent aspect of hardwiring, each design displays specific motor skill traits. Region I Empathetic Sensates tend to incorporate their entire body into activity, due to their gross-motor dominance. From sweeping the floor to lifting boxes to swinging a tennis racket or golf club, this can be evident.

Analytic Sensates (Region II), with their fine-motor hardwiring proficiency, may often display excellent hand-eye coordination and be more "handsy" and "wristy" in their movements. As we move further down the motor cortex, away from region I and the gross motors, we find less big-muscle incorporation with region III Empathetic Conceptuals and especially with region IV Analytic Conceptuals. Region III EC designs, however, may incorporate a combination of both the big muscles and fine motors better than most.

Left-brainers will be more deliberate—almost "mechanical"—in their movements, while Right-brainers will be more free-flowing and "loosey-goosey." Front-brainers will tend to move in a more high-energy fashion, while Back-brainers have a tendency to be more energy-conserving in their activity.

This is just a small sample of the many clues that can lead to proper identification of one's specific hardwired design, so let's take a closer look at each one.

Sensates

Though the eight hardwired Sensate designs are separated into two separate motor skill groups (Region I gross-motor dominant ES and region II fine-motor dominant AS), hemisphere dominance also plays a significant factor in differentiating these here-and-now people.

Right-brained Sensates (RS)
(I-1 FRES, I-2 BRES, II-1 FRAS, II-2 BRAS)

The four RS designs may seem to have very little in common upon initial examination. Closer inspection, however, will reveal the similarities. For instance, a meticulous dentist and a daredevil racecar driver both use *tools* to do their job—a practice to which the RS is naturally drawn. Both may be skilled in their seemingly very different crafts and both have a deep need to work with tools as an extension of themselves in these chosen professions.

Of course, at first glance these two people might well appear to be completely different. However, the innate inclination to use tools and employ the use of their extremities as a means of self-expression is consistent with the RS circuitry. These RS designs are found often among athletes, dancers, artists, mechanics, dentists, construction workers, and racers (all vocations which have some means of projecting their hardwired tendencies – athletic equipment, dance step, paintbrush, wrench, dentist drill, hammer/bulldozer, car/boat/plane/motorcycle, etc.). Athletics, with the various balls, bats, racquets, clubs, sticks, etc., are a natural outlet of expression for the RS.

The RS designs have an unmatched desire for freedom, action, independence, and opportunity. They want to set their own hours and work with those they like. With a natural love of travel, they want the freedom to enjoy life as it comes. The RS will show boldness by taking risks. This is not to say every RS is adventure-oriented, but most will be drawn to vocations that involve action, movement, and perhaps an occasional "thrill." Sitting behind a desk all day pushing papers will be a tough assignment for the RS.

The action-oriented RS likes to live for the moment, often at the expense of long-range planning. They may become restless if they see no hope for immediate action. Whether performing tirelessly before others or saving their strength for the next opportunity, RS people are conspicuous for their love of action for action's sake.

I must point out one cautionary note with regard to these high-energy, go-with-the-flow Right-brainers. While any design can be drawn to addictive drugs and alcohol, these action-oriented, live-for-the-moment risk-takers may be most vulnerable. They are also, incidentally, the most apt to get a tattoo or body piercing on the spur of the moment, only to regret it later.

Left-brained Sensates (LS)
(I-3 FLES, I-4 BLES, II-3 FLAS, II-4 BLAS)

The practical, dutiful, and faithful LS is the pillar of society. Dependable, industrious, and pragmatic, the LS values tradition and abides by the rules and standards of the social unit. Tireless workers, LS designs prefer to be known as *givers* as opposed to takers. Often content to maintain a low profile, the LS may prefer to work for the benefit of others. They feel obligated to serve and may feel uncomfortable when on the receiving end.

LS designs are drawn to the world through their five senses. They are generally at home in the arena where facts, numbers and details are of concern. As for the knowledge of products and their usefulness, none is better in judging quality than the observant LS.

Generally commerce-oriented, pragmatic and independent, the LS believes that hard work is necessary to earn rewards. Work must precede play, and the rule is generally not to be broken. LS people have a tendency to become over-worked, as they find it tough to refuse added responsibility. They are easily prone to taking on more than they can possibly accomplish, which can lead to a state of depression as they feel the weight of their many obligations.

The LS is a guardian of time-honored institutions. They value, support and perpetuate the home, social club, church, company and country. They like to be prepared and may be considered very "protective." This may lead them to become somewhat pessimistic at times, prompting them to prepare for the worst.

Conceptuals

Conceptuals live in the world of *possibilities* more so than their Sensate counterparts. **C**s live with a quest for finding purpose and meaning in their lives. They are the ones who will be most often found in the self-help section of the local bookstore.

Just as with Sensates, the Left/Right brain difference has an impact, though it is not quite so pronounced when it comes to behavior and thought process. This is perhaps due to the "possibility-thinking" of the dominant **C**.

However, the impact of the Empathetic vs. Analytic mindset can be clearly felt among the Conceptual designs. Therefore, we consider these dyads from a different point of comparison than their Sensate counterparts.

Empathetic Conceptuals (EC)
(III-1 FREC, III-2, BREC, III-3 FLEC, III-4 BLEC)

The EC has a strong regard for the feelings and rights of people. They feel a strong kinship with their fellow man and value relationships. ECs take great pride in the tasks they perform and thrive on the acknowledgment and recognition of a job well done.

These naturally optimistic Conceptuals tend to assume the best in others, due to their Empathetic wiring. They may often be found serving in roles that aid in the well-being of others, such as educators, ministers, counselors, and health-oriented professionals. With a natural flair for the spoken and written word, ECs are also supportive communicators. It is not surprising that the Front-brained ECs excel with oral communication while their Back-brained counterparts gravitate to the more subtle written word. As creative wordsmiths, ECs may be found penning innovative journalistic ideas in the form of drama, poetry, fiction, and psychology. There are many EC theologians.

As Empathetic people, ECs naturally place harmony in relationships as a high priority. They place tactfulness above truthfulness in relationships and will use their skills to maintain these relationships, accordingly. As abstract, theoretical Conceptuals, ECs enjoy tackling complex global issues. It is not uncommon to find ECs among the ranks of National Merit Finalists, Valedictorians, and Rhodes Scholars, alongside their Analytic counterparts.

Because ECs take great pride in their competence when it comes to people-oriented issues, they may not handle criticism well, leading to a drop in productivity if they become disheartened.

Analytic Conceptuals (AC)
(IV-1 FRAC, IV-2 BRAC, IV-3 FLAC, IV-4 BLAC)

As Conceptuals, ACs tend to focus on possibilities. Unlike their Empathetic counterparts, however, Analytics naturally incorporate impersonal logic in their thought process, as opposed to more subjective "feeling." ACs are the technically-oriented scientists who acquire knowledge by probing and investigating before thoughtfully contemplating their findings.

ACs naturally score high on IQ tests and can easily do well in academics with the proper discipline. Blessed with an innate giftedness for gaining intelligence, ACs may find they can get by in school without extensive study habits. A student who gets relatively poor grades yet amazes others with accompanying high scores on standardized tests is most likely an undisciplined AC.

As Analytic logicians, ACs may have a tendency to carry logic to extremes, leading to high expectations of themselves and others. Often oblivious to the feelings of others, this may lead to criticism of another's lack of understanding something that seems quite evident. Often their own toughest critic, they may not feel a need to seek approval from others, nor be inclined to give it, as competence is expected in anything to which they put their mind. ACs tend to become absorbed in their work, often "burning the midnight oil," as they work late into the night, showing little sign of fatigue.

As they ponder problems in their inquisitive mind, ACs may often have the appearance of being disinterested in others' emotions. Rather than disregarding others, however, this trait may be more accurately described as an innate preoccupation with their own fertile thoughts. They would much rather spend time with their own thoughts than with other people if they don't find sufficient value in what others have to offer.

Methodical, ingenious, and naturally inquisitive, ACs are often found in areas requiring the skillful adaptation of knowledge to problems. Curious, precocious, and inventive, ACs are often found in the worlds of computer programming and analysis, engineering, law, design, architecture, medicine, the sciences, and any other field that requires creative, strategic thought. As complex thinkers and problem-solvers, ACs do not find much satisfaction in accomplishing routine tasks.

9

Region
I
Empathetic Sensates

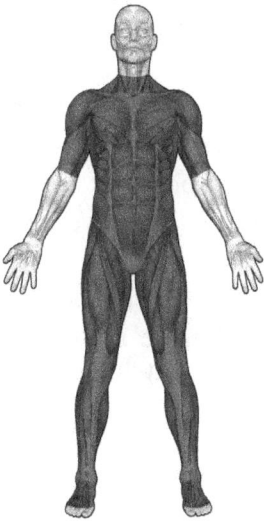

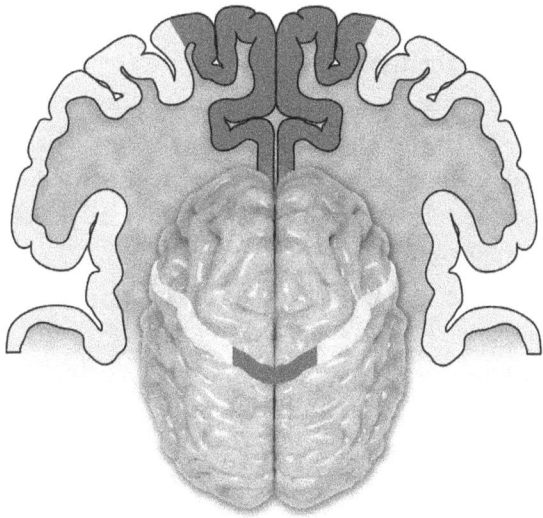

Region I - Empathetic Sensates
Gross-Motor Skilled

Empathetic Sensates are pragmatic, personable people. As "feeling" Es and observant Sensates, they are very aware of others' feelings, in addition to their own. As a result, they tend to really care what others think of them.

Gross-motor (big muscle) skilled, they rely more on the large muscles for body movements than any of the other body skill groups. This can often be observed clearly in athletics and even in mundane tasks such as swatting a fly, sweeping the floor or shoveling dirt, snow, etc.

Personal Observers are generally known for being peacemakers. They would rather get along than fight unnecessarily. They usually embody the essence of treating others the way they would want to be treated themselves.

ESs are by and large friendly, down-to-earth people who are very much focused on the here-and-now. The abstract world is not to their liking. They are often service-oriented in their vocations: nurses, salespeople, counselors, teachers, real estate agents, social workers, athletes, and religious workers.

One other note regarding the region I Empathetic Sensate designs: ESs will tend to slur their words, or mumble more than anyone. This may be due to the fact that their motor skill strengths are concentrated on the big muscles—the region on the motor cortex farthest away from the mouth and tongue.

I-1 FRES — "Social Performer"

FRONT, RIGHT-BRAIN (Q1), EMPATHETIC, SENSATE

(quickly explores and responds to observations personally)

Order of Function Dominance: *SENSING*, EMPATHETIC, Analytic, conceptual

Appearance

"Look at me" is the heart's cry of the outgoing, fun-loving I-1 FRES, who can often be found wearing the latest style adorned with lots of jewelry. Dressed like "a million"—whether they have it or not—the FRES sees vivid clothing as a means of self-expression. Females will frequently feature long, colorfully painted finger nails.

This naturally flamboyant inclination shows itself with a tendency for going a bit too far at times. Whether excessive makeup, too many sparkles, a wild hairdo, or extremely bright colors, the FRES dresses to impress! FRES females may be drawn to the opposite extreme, as well, showing a tendency toward skimpy outfits that reveal a conspicuous amount of flesh.

While some hardwired designs understand we must "eat to live," the FRES "lives to eat." As dominant Sensates, they love to enjoy the pleasing aroma and tastes of various foods. Combined with their naturally social nature, this can lead them to unhealthy diets, vulnerable to both poor choices and excessive quantities. As a result, they can be prone to be overweight to some degree, in spite of their naturally active nature. Females are normally naturally curvy, which is only enhanced by this dieting tendency.

Personality

The FRES loves life and people. Entertaining and fun-loving, they seek attention and enjoyment in all they do. They thrive on being in front of others, displaying their natural showmanship.

If not having fun, their attitude may quickly go south. Typically energetic, gregarious, sociable, charming, and generous, they see gifts as symbols of love and affection. As such, they enjoy giving them almost as much as receiving. The FRES is one of the most naturally generous designs. Normally energetic and boisterous, they love to give hugs, naturally incorporating the big muscles into their interactions with others.

Though normally good-natured, easy going, and affable, the FRES is particularly sensitive in the emotional center of the right brain, which can often lead to being quick tempered. When FRES children get upset, it may be impossible to reason with them until they calm down. They can just as quickly regain their composure, however, and are not ones to hold a grudge.

Generally unconcerned with details, the FRES can be audacious, daring, and spontaneous. Virtually any environment is a makeshift stage for these lively, impulsive performers. Light-hearted, romantic, and optimistic, the FRES has an innate need to feel the love and care of others, perhaps more than any other hardwired design.

Extremely literal, the dominate Sensing FRES is not prone to deep thinking, especially regarding issues that don't involve people. With a knack for dealing well with the practical, immediate facts of life, the FRES normally displays a good measure of common sense, especially when relaxed and thinking calmly. When their emotions get amped up, however, they can be prone to spur-of-the-moment decision-making that they may later well regret. The FRES is perhaps the most apt to come home baring a tattoo they had no intention of getting when they left the house. They may also be drawn to body art as another way of attracting attention.

Children

FRES children are natural bundles of hyperactivity, constantly messing up the house, being loud, and always wanting to do one more thing. They love surprises, both giving and receiving. They long to be the center of attention, whether it be during family time around the dinner table, or putting on a "show" in the living room. The FRES relishes the excitement of performing for others.

This high-energy design is the definition of a kinesthetic learner. The FRES greatly prefers doing over watching. Though they may not naturally take to the rudimentary atmosphere of elementary school, when they can touch, taste, feel, or otherwise experience the lesson to be learned, they will not only be content, but will thrive. Hating to see anything fun come to an end, they love to do things "one more time."

The dominant Sensing FRES lives life in the moment. They

I-1 FRES Traits

Appearance
- decorated
- inviting
- lots of jewelry
- prone to be overweight to some degree
- dresses to impress / be noticed
- vivid clothing (often a means of self-expression)
- often long, colorfully painted finger nails (women)

Personality
- energetic, boisterous, loud, love to give hugs (incorporate the big muscles)
- entertaining, fun-loving
- affectionate, caring
- light hearted, romantic, optimistic
- good-natured, easy going, affable
- sympathetic, empathetic, bighearted and generous
- unconcerned with details
- audacious, daring, spontaneous and impulsive
- capricious and whimsical
- quick-tempered

Athletic Characteristics
- superior gross-motor fluidity and body balance
- excellent reaction time
- fluid, strong, aggressive
- not afraid of contact
- unrestrained, free-flowing, go-for-it mentality
- graceful
- daring, crowd-pleasing
- chatty, reactionary, spontaneous
- offensive-minded
- often breaks the rules of the game (detests constricting "rules" to begin with)

want to have their cake and eat it, too—*now!* FRES students enjoy learning things and skills that can be applied immediately. Trade schools are often filled with this design. When it comes to learning facts, the FRES loves lists, such as memorizing states, capitols, etc. As secondary Empathetics, they also love unusual facts involving people. The *Guinness Book of World Records* can often be found on the bookshelf of the young FRES.

Athletic Characteristics

Arguably the top athletic hardwired design, the Right-brained FRES displays superior gross-motor fluidity and body balance. Even a large FRES will display excellent reaction speed and first-step quickness. Fluid, strong, and aggressive, the FRES is generally not afraid of contact. They live life with their graceful body (more than the mind), implementing an unrestrained, free-flowing, go-for-it mentality.

As dominant Sensates, they possess superior peripheral and stereoscopic Right-brained vision, which provides them with an innate athletic advantage. FRES athletes are naturally hardwired to have among the best field and court-awareness, instinctively knowing the location of both teammates and the ball.

The FRES is a daring design, willing to take chances to make a crowd-pleasing play. Wired with the ability to make spontaneous decisions, they often excel without even knowing how they did it. Ask the FRES after a game how they were able to make the "big play" and prepare to receive an answer much more vague and general than from some other designs.

Offensive-minded, the FRES detests rules and structure, though they do aim to please their coaches. They easily become bored with training that features mindless repetition. They just want to play, even if it's only practice. Make it a game and you have their attention. They also thrive on rewards for reaching goals, both individually, and as a team. With a spontaneous, Sensing mindset, the FRES performs best in an unrestricted environment.

A restrictive, regimented game plan not only hinders the play of this naturally creative design, but also puts this reactionary athlete into "thinking" mode, which is extremely debilitating. A simple game plan that allows for a reasonable amount of freelancing will provide the optimal environment for this gifted athlete to perform at the highest level.

Popular Vocations

The FRES is drawn to careers involving people, as well as jobs where they can use their body. Athletics is a natural fit, providing a venue in which to use their smooth big-muscle proficiency, along with the opportunity to perform for the crowd.

FRESs are natural conciliators and mediators, able to adroitly balance issues and find points of agreement. They are skilled at personalizing their sales presentations to fit the needs of their listeners.

Sales, public relations, and counseling are among the relational occupations where they can often be found. FRESs work well with people in a crisis situation. Genuinely sensitive and compassionate, they are actively concerned for the welfare of others.

Vocations that provide an atmosphere in which results can be seen immediately are also popular, such as auto mechanic, transportation, carpentry, and construction. Design, cosmetology, catering, nursing, and child care are other areas that are natural fits.

Using their body, helping people, and doing things that can be appreciated by the five senses are all common themes in the life of the I-1 FRES.

Well-Known FRES Designs

Think about "living life with your body" and the first entertainer that may come to mind, for those old enough to remember, is **Elvis Presley**. "The King," of course, made news in his early years, as television cameras were ordered to only show him from the waist up, lest the American viewing audience be subjected to his body-twisting and shaking ways!

Dolly Parton is another classic FRES, whose body (think big hair, big smile, and other big "stuff") has been as much a part of her "big personality" and celebrity as her amazing voice. Basketball's **Magic Johnson** and his classic light-up-the-room smile personifies the FRES, while **LeBron James** and MLB's **Ken Griffey Jr.** are two more examples of great gross-motor dominant athletes who exemplify what it means to have *fun* playing the game. That certainly describes the FRES design at its best!

Others who displayed the athletic giftedness of the FRES design include **Barry Bonds, Serena Williams,** and the legendary **Muhammad Ali.**

Performance Keys

The I-1 FRES is inherently impulsive, drawn to having fun in the moment, regardless of the activity. For this Empathetic Right-brainer and dominant Sensate, tomorrow often seems like an eternity away, taking a back seat to the pleasure of today. This can lead to the FRES easily becoming distracted, leaving tasks undone. It can also lead to spending money they don't have, or at least failing to set funds aside for the future.

Making thorough, organized plans and dutifully sticking to them will be a helpful skill that will enable this fun-loving design to avoid regret later. Setting goals, both long-range and short-term, will also help to maintain focus. Being especially mindful of how long-term consequences can be impacted by impulsive short-term decisions is a vital practice. Learning to slow down and use logical analysis when making decisions is a discipline that will pay a lifetime of dividends.

As an Empathetic "people person," the FRES design is inherently generous. Combined with their love of "things" that comes from being dominant Sensates, they like to give gifts—the bigger the better—to others, as well as to themselves. This contributes to being more of a natural spender than a saver. Learning to appreciate the long-term value of saving over the short-term attraction of spending is a very beneficial discipline to acquire.

It is also good to be cognizant that more is not always better, be it with food, jewelry, or cosmetics.

I-2 BRES — "Harmonious Free Spirit"

BACK, RIGHT-BRAIN (Q2), EMPATHETIC, SENSATE

(deeply compares and appraises personal observations)

Order of Function Dominance: *EMPATHETIC*, SENSING, Conceptual, analytic

Appearance

As the Back-brained counterpart of the FRES, the I-2 BRES is similar in many ways, though more subdued, as would be expected. The BRES is also a lover of colorful, visually pleasing clothes and accessories, yet will not be as apt to go overboard in quantity or flair. Female BRES designs will be particularly fond of making an artful expression with their outfit.

The BRES features a warm, yet somewhat shy smile. An artistic look may accompany what is normally a tranquil and peaceful aura about them. Being Back-brained, the BRES may have a tendency for making lesser eye contact around strangers.

As dominant Empathetics, they have a natural love of animals. The Back-brained BRES may be content to sit and hold or pet a small animal for what seems to be an inordinate length of time.

Personality

Unlike the FRES, who is a dominant Sensate, the BRES is hardwired with Empathy as its dominant function. As such, the BRES has an artistic feel for handling interpersonal relationships. Typically humble, reflective, kind, harmonious, and fun-loving, BRESs feature a naturally sweet-spirited disposition that makes them a joy to be around. With a sympathetic and calm demeanor, the BRES has a quiet adoration of people, especially children.

Lovers of nature, they also relate well to animals, and can often be found beautifying the environment. Naturally service-oriented, the BRES is drawn to the aid of the less fortunate, taking joy in caring for the needs of others.

As much as the BRES is innately pleasant and caring, these sensitive emotions can be fragile. Easily prone to mood swings, this sensitive design thrives with gentle, loving encouragement.

Impulsive, curious, and visual, the free-flowing BRES detests constricting schedules. Living in the moment, they appreciate life's simple pleasures and value free time for leisure. These leisure time pursuits will, not surprisingly, involve anything sensory and visual, such as photography, art, music, dance, sports, clothing, and food.

The BRES admires beauty, color, and texture. To express themselves, they may turn to action, intricate gift making, and crafts.

Quiet and kind, the BRES tends to have a large group of friends who are attracted to this easy to get along with personality. Peacemakers by nature, they promote harmony and avoid disagreements whenever possible. With a dominant Empathetic sense of the needs and feelings of others, the BRES strives to lend a hand. This constant natural interaction leads to building many friendly relationships.

Children

BRES children are innately self-deprecating, often lacking self-confidence and naturally shrugging off praise. They may be the most humble and misunderstood of all hardwired designs, prone to underestimating their own abilities and achievements.

A dominant Empathetic, the fragile emotions of the sensitive young BRES can be prone to mood swings. They are vulnerable to depression and may need frequent encouragement. With confidence-boosting affirmation, however, their artistic and social giftedness will blossom.

Though others may be drawn to the quiet, kind, easy-to-live-with BRES, this reticent design will generally be found with only a handful of close friends early in life. The BRES values leisure time to enjoy life's simple pleasures, often working by themselves outside.

In school, the BRES requires a friendly, harmonious environment. Their desire to learn will be quickly discouraged by an impersonal instructor. The BRES often has difficulty grasping complex ideas initially, requiring repetition in order gain an understanding of abstract subject matter.

While they can do fine in school, BRES children are generally not considered good test-takers. As a dominant Empathetic and Right-brained Sensate, the BRES has difficulty accessing Conceptual intuition and logic when feeling stress. They can easily blank on a test or when questioned verbally in front of the class. When they know their subject well, however, the BRES can excel on exams, especially

I-2 BRES Traits

Appearance
- artistic look, a tranquil and peaceful aura
- warm but shy smile
- clothing comfy and visually pleasing (via color or tasteful style) as an artful expression (women)
- humble countenance
- deliberate speech
- lesser eye contact

Personality
- sweet spirited
- good-natured, playful, fun-loving
- easy going, relaxed, agreeable, freedom-seeking
- may be easily manipulated, often naïve
- sympathetic, calm, quietly loving people
- creative and artistic
- service-oriented
- meek, docile, may be unmotivated
- sensitive, stubborn
- loves children

Athletic Characteristics
- superior gross-motor fluidity and body balance
- coordinated, graceful
- slightly deliberate
- amenable to coaching
- may need encouragement for expending the necessary energy game after game
- tactical
- plays within rules unless finding an opportunity to get away with not doing so

when limited Analytic reasoning is required.

Athletic Characteristics

As with the FRES, the similarly Right-brained BRES possesses superior gross-motor fluidity and body balance. Coordinated and graceful, the BRES is a smooth and artistic athlete. Closely in tune with their body, they enjoy the feelings they get from graceful movement, naturally performing with smooth elegance and strength.

As energy conserving Back-brainers, the BRES may seem passive until the game starts. Between the lines, however, they can become as competitive as any design. With proper encouragement, the energy of the BRES can be extended long after others have faded. Often synonymous with the "long-lasting Energizer bunny," they may use their ES gross-motor dominance to continue playing and working long after their contemporaries have retired to the proverbial rocking chair.

The BRES performs best when deep-thinking analysis is not mandated. They naturally handle pressure using gut-level instincts and the synthetic reasoning of the Right brain. They also possess exceptional Sensate, Right-brained peripheral and stereoscopic vision, providing them with an additional advantage on the playing field.

The reserved and harmonious BRES can often be a mystery to coaches who look for an energetic and aggressive temperament, especially in practice. The BRES is not one who naturally seeks to "destroy" the opponent. When the competition becomes heated, however, their Back-brained Empathetic function can drive them to become intense and driven. The outwardly calm demeanor of the BRES athlete belies the intense emotion driving them from within.

Popular Vocations

The dependable and hard-working BRES is drawn to practical, hands-on trades. They work visually with their environments and prefer disciplines in which they can serve others or help to beautify their surroundings. While speaking in front of groups may not come naturally, the BRES relates well one-on-one and with small groups, appealing to others with their friendly and helpful demeanor.

They may be found in nursing, child care, animal care, ministry, and any vocation devoted to helping others. They also are frequent in athletics, art, and dance, where their graceful talent freely comes alive. Music, photography, construction, and farming are other areas where their physical artistry and love of nature can be readily incorporated.

The BRES is not normally attracted to selling tangible goods, but can team up with others to find success in sales. Seeking to serve rather than to receive from others, they are naturally hesitant to push in order to close the deal. In sales, they do best with products and services they truly believe will benefit the customer.

The BRES is a reliable teammate and friendly co-worker. Finding the repetitive structure of a daily routine boring and confining, they flourish in an environment that offers freedom and spontaneity.

Well-Known BRES Designs

Television personality and animal enthusiast **"Jungle Jack" Hanna** personifies the BRES male. He gained a reputation as a zealously hard worker in his early days as director of the Columbus Zoo, where he would reportedly walk around personally picking up trash in the hours after closing. His genial demeanor in television appearances with *Johnny Carson*, *Good Morning America* and *David Letterman* gained national notoriety for both himself and the zoo.

The long-lasting nature of the BRES was exemplified by "Mr. Hockey" **Gordie Howe**. The 23-time All-Star maintains the NHL record for most games and seasons played. His 26-year NHL career does not even include six more seasons spent in the rival WHA! Howe finally retired from full-time competition at age 52!

Even in a high-energy sport like basketball, the BRES can keep going when others have lost their legs. **Robert Parish** finally retired at 43 years old in 1997 as the NBA's all-time leader in games played.

Dr. Tom Amberry demonstrated BRES big-muscle dominance and Back-brained concentration in 1993 when he set the world record for consecutive free throws made—at the age of 70! Amberry made 2,750 free throws without a miss over a 12-hour period. His streak was only snapped by time when they finally turned out the lights at the public gymnasium in which he was shooting!

15-time NBA All-Star **Tim Duncan** personified the quiet

intensity of the BRES competitor before retiring in 2016, ranked eighth all-time in games played.

Performance Keys

The I-2 BRES naturally possesses a generally quiet, soft-spoken demeanor. This may lead to difficulty with self-expression, especially verbally. Speaking in front of groups can be especially daunting to this naturally reserved design. Emulating the boldness of the closely related FRES is a good way to overcome apprehension with verbal expression. Given time and repetition, the people-oriented BRES will learn to enjoy and look forward to sharing their message with others.

Even in more intimate settings, it is helpful to keep in mind that there are, indeed, times when it is appropriate to speak up. The BRES should be encouraged to do so with confidence, especially when it comes to sharing feelings. Blessed with a high degree of emotional intelligence, the dominant Empathetic BRES may well contribute an important perspective to the conversation.

Just as with the FRES, perseverance and sticking to the task at hand is difficult at times, especially when it involves a project that is not enjoyable. Incorporating logical analysis into decision-making and visualizing the long-term consequences of short-term actions can be beneficial. Constructing a pre-planned schedule can aid in this process by providing the organization mechanism that does not come naturally to this free-flowing design.

I-3 FLES — "Personable Provider"

FRONT, LEFT-BRAIN (Q3), EMPATHETIC, SENSATE
(critiques, acts on, and communicates personal observations)
Order of Function Dominance: *EMPATHETIC*, SENSING, Conceptual, analytic

Appearance

As the most innately sociable of all the hardwired designs, the I-3 FLES displays a naturally warm, cheerful appearance. A bright smile is normally complimented with a strong, verbally expressive voice. Like all Empathetic Sensates, the FLES has a strong sense of fashion and will be found more often than not carefully dressed in colorful, yet uncomplicated, versions of the latest styles.

Left-brain dominance drives the FLES to be naturally organized. They take comfort in the plan that a schedule provides, both for themselves, as well as for those around them. Traditional and family-minded, they will show respect for customs of their culture, both in appearance and decor.

They tend to give good eye contact, due to their Front-brained hardwiring, as well as their powerful Empathetic drive to interact with others.

Personality

Natural hosts and hostesses, the FLES has a knack for taking care of others. With a hospitable, welcoming persona, they have an innate focus on being useful. FLESs converse readily with others, sharing a positive, optimistic outlook as they mingle with an easy confidence at social functions. Caring and always ready to lend a hand, the FLES is an excellent listener, as well. With a sympathetic heart and a practical outlook on life, the FLES finds it easy to provide counsel in a simple, conversationalist manner. They are devoted friends, using their Front-brained Empathy to maintain a wide array of relationships.

At least one FLES is needed at most social gatherings, although the I-1 FRES ranks a close second. The FLES will be a little more organized, the FRES a little more entertaining. Both designs will exude warmth. The FLES naturally organizes the parties and is devoted to making everyone glad they came.

Friendly and outgoing, the conscientious FLES is energized by being with other people. They are "energy givers," infecting those around them with their natural vitality. This high energy level enables them to put in long hours on the job, as well. However, this same energy used to help make others' day go smooth can leave the FLES physically exhausted by the end of the day.

The FLES values harmony, putting the feelings of others first and foremost in decision making. They readily express admiration and appreciate when affirmation is similarly returned.

When tough times hit, the FLES may fear the worst. As people of action, they will strive to personally solve the problem, even if it is not theirs to solve. The hard-working, decision-oriented FLES sees a need and is naturally driven to action. Completion without delay is their mantra.

Children

The young FLES is outgoing, rule following, and socially adept, drawn to people and social interaction. FLESs thrive on being around others, naturally leading, relating, and conversing with ease. They love to share their experiences and ideas, and relish having time for activity and friends. As naturally organized Left-brainers, however, FLESs are inclined to see that work is done before they can genuinely enjoy leisure time.

As with all Empathetic Sensates, the FLES prefers learning and dealing with facts over abstract concepts. They can be over-achievers in school, driven to please both teachers and parents. A good relationship with the teacher is vital to the learning process for the FLES, who also appreciates an organized classroom structure. Hands-on, experiential activities, especially with committee-oriented interaction, provide an optimal learning environment.

Conservative by nature, FLESs are not risk-takers. They are characterized by their self-discipline, caring, and energetic way of living.

Athletic Characteristics

As a region I Empathetic Sensate, the FLES is naturally gross-motor skilled and can be very athletic. Being Left-brain dominant, however, this big-muscle proficiency is more deliberate and planned

I-3 FLES Traits

Appearance
- warm, cheerful
- verbally expressive, strong voice
- bright smiling
- carefully dressed and colorful
- usually modest, uncomplicated
- organized
- traditional
- gives eye contact

Personality
- social butterfly
- positive, optimistic, constructive
- very feeling and emotional, a hugger
- orderly, instructional, diligent
- caring, ready to lend a hand
- values harmony and feelings
- practical
- energetic and conscientious
- hospitable, welcoming, focused on being useful
- simple conversationalist, forthcoming, talkative
- driven, hopeful, Pollyanna.

Athletic Characteristics
- superior gross-motor control and body balance
- hard worker
- energetic but slow moving, mechanical
- timid, injury prone
- good body balance
- deliberate, planned, defensive-minded
- good with logistics
- team builder
- may give up too soon
- plays by the rules unless feelings are hurt

than the smooth, synthetic actions of their Right-brained counterparts. Playing with the same high-energy trait that characterizes their persona, they nevertheless are slower-moving, due to their sequential big-muscle dominance.

The Left brain also encourages a more planned, defensive-minded style of play. FLESs are good team builders, naturally supporting teammates with vocal encouragement. Though generally positive competitors, they may be apt to easily throw in the towel if things are not going their way.

With a natural aversion to sports and activities that instill fear, the FLES is more commonly found in sports such as basketball, tennis, golf, swimming, and figure skating.

Popular Vocations

As the most sociable of all hardwired designs, and skillful at promoting harmony among others, FLESs are a welcome addition to any business establishment. The highly energetic FLES can best be described as a "friendly facilitator." With a fervor for relationships, the FLES complements the business world with honesty and good-natured policies. They naturally put the needs of the customer or employee first, earning the confidence needed to make the sale, as well as making them agreeable managers and employers.

FLESs are friendly and demonstrative, deriving energy simply from mingling with people. It seems their batteries never need charging as they vivaciously go about their work. In the company of others, FLESs almost always have something to offer in the way of words.

The accommodating, people-minded FLES is, of course, drawn to service occupations. They may often be found in nursing, social services, ministry, secretarial, counseling, child care, and teaching—especially at the elementary school level. They can also be successful motivational speakers, winning over the audience with their caring demeanor, practical examples, and social sophistication.

Friendly and demonstrative, it may seem they never need a break, as they continuously go about their work in a vivacious fashion. With a strong knack for interior decorating and clothing style, the FLES specializes in hosting and making things more practical. They seek immediate usefulness in their work, striving for orderliness and structure.

Well-Known FLES Designs

The late **Princess Diana** exemplified the FLES design. Uncomfortable with the limelight that came with being Princess of Wales, "Lady Di" found that she could use her position to advance the work of numerous causes dear to her. Before her untimely death, she was known for her work with charities and organizations that supported youths, the homeless, drug addicts, and the elderly. First Lady **Barbara Bush**, another FLES, also took an interest in helping the homeless, as she felt it a primary factor in her signature cause, illiteracy.

NFL Hall of Fame coach **Joe Gibbs** was widely known for his legendary work ethic, as well as being a devoted Christian and family man. It was not uncommon for him to spend days on end holed up in his office constructing a game plan for the upcoming game. Despite working round the clock with only periodic naps, Gibbs strived to keep up with his family. Believing that some of the best family discussions coincide with mealtime, Gibbs would have his wife record dinner-table conversation so that he could listen at work.[13]

In 1994, **Nancy Kerrigan** demonstrated the proficient gross-motor control of the FLES design as she combined balance and precision en route to the silver medal at the Winter Olympics.

Performance Keys

The dominant Empathetic function of the I-3 FLES drives an innate desire to continually care for the needs of others. This may often lead to high anxiety levels as the FLES strives to pack too much into the day, fearing the worst if it cannot be completed. Those hardwired with this caring design must realize and accept the fact that they may not be able to do it all. They must be willing to ask others to chip in and do their share.

In the workplace, it is imperative that the FLES has a job that entails regular contact with others. It is also important to find a career in a field of interest. Though not necessarily inclined to more technical work, so long as there interest in the job, the FLES will demonstrate an energetic determination to learn and do it well.

The FLES also has a tendency to want to plan and control everything around them, especially when it comes to the family. It is important to be accepting of the fact that things do not always go as planned. Appreciating the big picture and not getting hung up on little things will go a long way toward limiting stress. Focusing on the many good things in life can be instrumental in avoiding despondency when things don't go as expected or hoped for.

As a Left-brained Sensate, the FLES is vulnerable to tension under pressure during athletic competition. This will naturally cause the big muscles to tighten, leading to excessive control and rigidity. Practicing techniques to relax the mind will pay significant dividends.

When it comes to parenting, the FLES may seek to avoid conflict, leaving the spouse to handle the disciplining. With an innate desire for peace and happiness, FLESs have a natural tendency to pacify and compromise, placing the blame on themselves for problems that inevitably arise. It is imperative that the FLES be aware of this self-deprecating penchant.

While proper exercise is an important part of any health regimen, it is especially important for the action-oriented FLES. Naturally putting work before play, this duty-driven design may put exercise off in favor of the never-ending work they see before them. Needing not only the physical outlet for pent up energies, but also the mental break from the obligations they place upon themselves, regular exercise contributes to a healthy routine.

Finally, when it comes to health and personal appearance, these Left-brained Sensates may be too tough on themselves, as their Empathetic feelings believe things to be worse than they truly are. It is important for FLESs to avoid being too self-conscious. As with all designs, one's internal beauty and goodness is significant.

I-4 BLES — "Guardian"

BACK, LEFT-BRAIN (Q4), EMPATHETIC, SENSATE
(methodically classifies observations personally)
Order of Function Dominance: *SENSING*, EMPATHETIC, Analytic, conceptual

Appearance

The I-4 BLES is a modest, humble-looking person who normally appears impeccably dressed. Despite the ES knack for style and fashion, the Back-brained BLES will trend toward conservative attire with few "bells and whistles." With a careful, neat appearance, the BLES will share a warm, yet shy, smile, and will avoid frequent, extended eye contact.

Born with a servant's heart, the traditionally-minded BLES will often be found working behind the scenes. With a Left-brained orderly mindset, they keep their workplace and home tidy and organized. As Back-brained Empathetic Sensates, they also have a good feel for value in material goods and are quite thrifty.

Their dutiful work ethic is complemented with a straightforward communication method that makes them valued, if underappreciated, members of any organization. Although generally reserved, especially in group settings, when they do speak up, it is with a deliberate and plain-spoken manner.

In the comfort of the family environment, some BLESs may develop what appears to be an energetic Front-brained persona, especially if surrounded by high-energy **F** family members. This apparent similarity to the closely related FLES will be exposed, however, when they venture out into the world. Their naturally lower energy level will become apparent, especially when it comes to talking and otherwise communicating with others.

Personality

The BLES is a true homebody. Whether alone or with close family, they value their downtime at home. Naturally modest, their deep values and firm loyalties serve as a foundation for a quiet, service-oriented mindset. They strive to cater to the needs of others and abhor leaving work unfinished. As rule-followers, they naturally stick to the guidebook while focused on working alone. They live by the mantra that work is good and must come before play. As such, they may have a tendency to become overworked.

They are very conscientious, devoted to family and raising their children to conform to the general norms of society. Because of this, they are prone to be judgmental toward nonconformists whose behavior and beliefs contradict that of the tradition-minded BLES. Though hesitant to speak up in a group setting, they may be much more inclined to engage in one-on-one gossip, as they share their feelings of indignation with a trusted friend or colleague.

As Empathetic Sensates, they prefer keeping life simple, and their Left-brained dominance leaves them resistant to change. Accordingly, they are not at the forefront of revolutions. They may lament the dawn of the computer era that has led to an ever-changing world. If you know someone who originally resisted getting a cell phone and later hung on to their flip phone dearly (as smart phones took over the market), you may know a BLES!

Though people-oriented Empathetics, the BLES generally maintains only a small circle of close friends, which they tend to maintain for their lifetime. The Back-brained BLES can sometimes resemble a Front-brainer when in a comfortable setting with people they know well. However, their lower innate energy level will be exposed soon enough as they lack the energy and talkativeness of their FLES counterparts.

As a Q4 Back, Left-brainer, the BLES may have a tendency to dwell on the negative in life, causing undue worry. Whether it be concern for their family, the future, or their safety, the BLES often carries the burdens of others. This excessive worrying can result in a "gloom and doom" mentality.

Children

Perhaps the most inherently compliant of all hardwired designs, BLESs make parenting seem easy. Undemanding and aiming to please, the young BLES possesses a pleasant, genial demeanor. Content to play alone, they also fit easily in groups, wearing a ready smile, satisfied to watch the activities of others.

They are orderly and obedient, completing their homework and doing their chores, even if not in the most energetic fashion. Dutiful

I-4 BLES Traits

Appearance
- impeccable in dress (conservative)
- modest, humble looking
- careful and neat
- conservatively warm smile
- deliberate and uncomplicated speech
- few "bells or whistles"
- traditional
- found in the background

Personality
- reserved but approachable
- generally humble
- shy, takes time to open up
- traditional
- observant
- kind, agreeable, amiable, cooperative
- patient, supportive, very helpful, loyal
- consistent, dependable, loyal, responsible
- good listener
- keeps to self
- self-effacing, gentle, feelings hurt easily
- hospitable, keenly aware of others and concerned with their welfare

Athletic Characteristics
- superior gross-motor control and body balance
- deliberate and mechanical movements
- defensive, restrained, timid
- very teachable
- agreeable with fellow athletes
- plays well within the rules of the game and acknowledges upon breaking one

students, BLESs enjoy practical subjects taught by organized teachers. They need clear expectations and sufficient time to meet them. As Back-brained energy-conservers, they may be prone to procrastinate without the proper encouragement.

Though they need time alone to recharge, they value their time with close friends and family. They epitomize loyalty, making it a point to keep in touch when others may have long since drifted apart. As Empathetic Sensates, being part of the learning process makes it much more meaningful. Field trips, experiments, and group projects are all preferable to navigating theoretical textbooks.

Athletic Characteristics

BLESs enjoy participating in sports, though they are rarely found reaching the professional ranks. Similar to their Q3 counterpart, the Left-brained Q4 BLES possesses deliberate and planned big-muscle control. Their Back-brained dominance, however, results in more restrained and timid defensive-minded actions.

The BLES is a good teammate, getting along well with fellow athletes. They are unselfish players, naturally seeking to play a complementary role to the more prolific members of the team.

Sports with naturally high fear factors are generally avoided by the BLES, whose generally timid and cautious nature carries over to the playing field. As Q4 specialists, they are naturally energy-conserving (Back-brain) and measured (Left-brain). In addition, as Empathetics, they seek harmony over contention. BLESs can learn to deal with these factors as they progress athletically, though they will always be factors in their game.

A naturally agreeable sort, the BLES is very teachable, studying the playbook and striving to please their coaches. They play well within the rules of the game, readily admitting their error should they should break one.

Popular Vocations

The BLES is naturally service-oriented, thriving on providing assistance to others. Often found working behind the scenes, the dedicated and painstaking BLES is normally a fine asset to any business. Despite this fact, they often go unnoticed, probably due to their relatively quiet dispositions. They are unlikely to grumble and complain while going about their work, at least publicly. BLESs are dedicated and committed workers, as long as they believe in the business in which they are working.

As Empathetics, BLESs enjoy working with people and are best suited for positions where there is the opportunity to be of benefit to the lives of others. They are often found in secretarial service, nursing, physical therapy, counseling, ministry, and social service work. Lovers of children and animals, they are also found in child care, veterinary work and teaching, especially at the elementary level.

Though not "born leaders," the dutiful BLES is often found working hard behind one. They are ideal employees in many ways, working hard for the cause in an effort to help make those around them better.

Well-Known BLES Designs

Because the behind-the-scenes BLES rarely seeks the limelight, not many are well known. Those who are generally become so through their participation in athletics. Perhaps the most prominent BLES in recent times is NFL quarterback **Carson Palmer**. In the testosterone-driven "he-man" world of professional football, Palmer stands out as a genuinely nice, self-deprecating person, who almost seems uncomfortable in the spotlight.

Walter Ray Williams, Jr. is the all-time leading money winner on the Pro Bowlers Association Tour, where he won over a third of his 47 PBA titles and six of his eight major after reaching the age of forty. However, the universally respected and popular PBA hall-of-famer earned the nickname "Deadeye" for his success in another sport. Williams is also a six-time Men's World Horseshoe Pitching champion. His longevity, as well as his renowned consistent accuracy across both sports, is a testament to the superior big-muscle control of this design.

Performance Keys

The dutiful I-4 BLES is compelled to complete the task at hand. However, an inherent unwillingness to adapt can oftentimes lead to struggles in today's ever changing world. The BLES must make it a priority to try new things and seek ways to be innovative within their realm of activity. This will not only reduce stress, but will prevent this tradition-minded design from falling behind as inevitable change occurs around them. BLES people must learn to accept when situations seem less than perfect.

Another helpful practice for the BLES is to seek ways to initiate new relationships. Making the time to engage in social activities will help the BLES to gain self-confidence, as they successfully interact with others. However, it is important that these energy-conserving Back-brainers not be too tough on themselves when they find they lack the stamina to keep up with the outgoing Front-brainers around them.

It is also helpful for these dominant Sensates to be mindful of a tendency to be caught up in the moment. Making long-range goals and being aware of the steps needed to reach them is an important self-discipline.

Because the BLES is so loyal and dutiful, they may be prone to being manipulated. To make it in the world, they may need to develop a toughness that allows them to speak up (and not just gossip) about any injustice to which they may be subjected.

Born with a gift of responsibility, the conscientious BLES naturally serves a vital support role in any organization, as well as in society in general. They should take pride in the knowledge that the quality and depth of their work makes up for the time they may take in getting it completed.

10
Region
II
Analytic Sensates

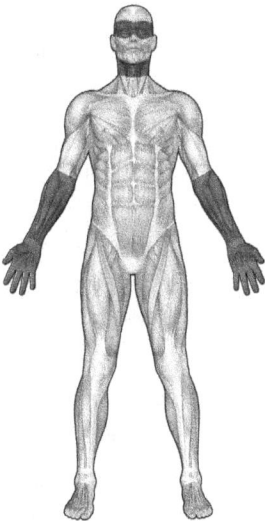

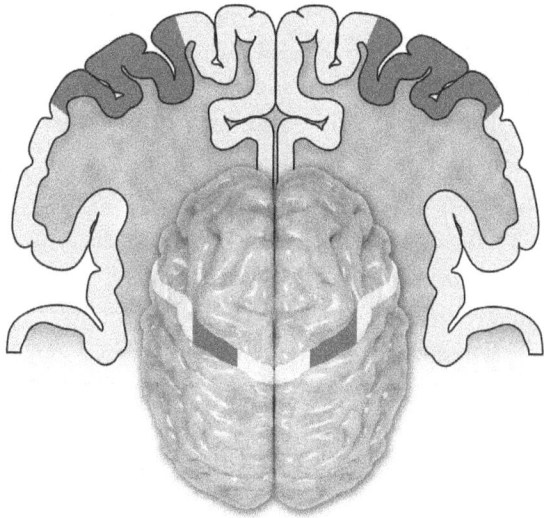

AS **Body Skill Group**
OBSERVE IMPERSONALLY

Region II - Analytic Sensates
Fine-Motor Skilled

Analytic Sensates are specialists at pragmatic logic. *They can often be spotted by their "hawk eyes," which may give them a piercing look.* This consistent correlation is due to the fact that these Impersonal "realists" are innately strongest in the hand-eye region of the brain and body. When they get serious or feel pressure, their eyes get intense and scrutinizing. The four region II AS designs have, by far, the most innately hawk-eyed appearance.

Not only do these designs develop superior hand-eye coordination and manual dexterity, but they can also have "vice grip"-like strength in their hands when needed. Their vision and spatial logic is extraordinary. When an AS says they see something, pay attention. Little escapes their notice!

By nature, AS people may not be very friendly, though they can learn to be. Their natural in-the-moment Analytical bent inclines them toward things over people.

Under pressure, their hands, wrists, and forearms can become too dominant, at the expense of effectively incorporating the big-muscle gross motors in their movements.

These Impersonal Observers are logical pragmatists in their vocations: they are accountants, financial consultants, securities brokers, lawyers, athletes, surgeons, salespeople, law enforcers, and so on. They are rarely involved in highly abstract or theoretical jobs.

II-1 FRAS — "Quarterback"

FRONT, RIGHT-BRAIN (Q1), ANALYTIC, SENSATE
(quickly explores and responds to observations impersonally)
Order of Function Dominance: *SENSING*, ANALYTIC, Empathetic, conceptual

Appearance

The II-1 FRAS is one of the most athletic, high-energy hardwired designs. As such, both males and females will tend to be well-built, featuring a shapely, muscular, even "chiseled" appearance. Females may have a slightly masculine tone, due to their "hard body" look and attitude. FRAS females gravitate toward action and independence. Even when they "settle down," they rarely fit the mold of the stereotypical housewife.

As might be expected with a design hardwired to give serious attention to their body, the dominant Sensing FRAS is also very clothes-conscious, often with a flamboyant flair. The clothing will normally be a relaxed, untailored look, yet they may well break out an outfit fashionably tailored for a special occasion. Odds are it will not be something conservative, as this daring, go-for-it design will not be hesitant to make a fashion statement. Conspicuous jewelry will often accompany the flashy attire, both for men, as well as women.

In addition to their attire and physique, their provocative and teasing nature often stands out in the crowd. Piercing AS "hawk eyes" can also sometimes be readily apparent in this design, which may be used to "stare down" a target or prospect.

Personality

A high-energy dynamo, the FRAS looks for excitement in everything they do. With an often hyperactive appearance, FRASs can have short attention spans as they search for the next big thing. They want to be on the go, experiencing as much as possible, and willing to try just about anything, at least once.

As smooth operators, they can work the room at social functions with flirtatious and sophisticated charm. They are natural promoters and entrepreneurs, with an uncanny ability to spot opportunity, just as a top quarterback can pick out his target in the midst of a field swarming with aggressive defenders. The innate self-centeredness of the FRAS, however, can lead to them being poor listeners.

Although naturally "street smart" and cunning, the FRAS may be impulsive and reckless. Their in-the-moment, go-for-it mentality can lead to trouble if they are not careful. As with all designs, upbringing can be an important factor in learning important habits and self-disciplines. For the FRAS, learning when and how to exercise self-control is critical. They can often be short-tempered and hotheaded.

While these are common traits, it is important to note that personas can vary widely for the FRAS, just as they can with all designs, at least to some degree. Some possessing the FRAS circuitry may appear reserved and uncommunicative, as their dominant Right brain fails to place a high value on the spoken word at times. They may prefer to rely more on their physical senses and actions. With careful observation, however, their behavior and performance should reveal the true innate design.

Children

The young FRAS can be both a joy to watch and a challenge to control. A bundle of energy, they relish exciting activity and the freedom to explore. Without that opportunity, their naturally short attention spans may suffer.

With a tendency for antics and nonconformity, the FRAS abhors the confinement of the mundane, traditional path. They are risk-takers and adventurers, drawn to tools and mechanical devices, including most anything with an engine—the more power, the better!

Young FRASs are not readers by nature, unless it involves a subject of great interest. They look for relevance, preferring fact over fiction. The study habits and organizational skills of the FRAS are generally lacking. Hardwired to be highly proficient in Q1, they are naturally inclined to go and act, as opposed to sit and organize.

Born with innate survival instincts, these natural salespeople win friends and supporters with their instinctive charm and charisma. They will do much for those they value, though without proper upbringing, they may well put themselves at the top of that list.

While not inherently trouble-makers, this freedom-loving design can easily be prone to mischief. They seek to impress others with

II-1 FRAS Traits

Appearance
- relaxed, untailored clothing (normally) yet may dress fashionably (even daringly) for the occasion
- jewelry not uncommon on men
- women are often slightly masculine or strong
- flamboyant, body and clothes conscious
- often well-built and in shape, muscular, hard look
- aggressive, provocative, teasing
- athletic
- AS "hawk eyes"

Personality
- risk-taking
- energetic yet in a stress-free way
- engaging the world, free-spirit
- usually active, athletic
- supreme realist, lives in the present
- speaks quickly and simply, not a conversationalist
- may be a poor listener, self-centered, self-directed
- egotistical, proud
- thrives on excitement
- impetuous, impulsive, may be foolhardy, reckless
- cunning, street smart, opportunistic
- entrepreneur, promoter
- often short-tempered, hotheaded

Athletic Characteristics
- superior hand-eye coordination (fine-motor positioning)
- strong upper body, tough-minded
- aggressive, operates at high gear, moves quickly
- highly tactical, though not a planner
- die-hard, powerful, "enforcer" mentality
- thrill-seeking, venturesome, antagonistic, hardliner
- deceptive, spontaneous, offensive-minded
- often breaks the rules of the game just to break them

their prowess or possessions, often placing the value of friends and entertainment above academics and rule-following.

Athletic Characteristics

Participating in sports can be a fine motivator for this superior athletic design. Not only will they be more inclined to adhere to rules and regulations, but it will encourage the learning thought process, as they seek excellence in their sport.

Hardwired in region II of the motor cortex, the fine-motor dominant FRAS possesses superior hand-eye coordination. Because they are drawn to sculpting their body, the FRAS athlete will generally not be lacking in strength. Usually super-aggressive on the field or court, FRASs may be characterized as playing with reckless abandon, especially at a young age. Eventually, however, they learn that controlled aggression is often required for ultimate success.

Though highly tactical, the FRAS is not a "planner" by nature. They perform best when reacting to the action in a spontaneous fashion. Any over-reliance on their Analytic "thinking" can quickly become debilitating, as it causes their naturally smooth fine-motor skills to become tight. They naturally take the field ready to play, requiring little time to warm up or get up to game speed.

While the FRAS is naturally hardwired for the quarterback position better than any other, this design is unwittingly being supplanted as today's game becomes increasingly complex. The more abstract and cerebral IV-1 FRAC is better able to grasp intricate, detailed pre-game *planning*, though remains no match for the quick-reacting FRAS in operating under pressure.

In addition to lightning-fast reactions, this dominant Sensing Right-brained Analytic design possesses extraordinary visual acuity and peripheral awareness. Their vision and spatial recognition under pressure is second to none.

The FRAS is an offensive-minded athlete, who will do whatever it takes to score. Willing to take chances that sometimes end up in disaster, more often these gutsy calls may lead to being heralded as the hero. As natural nonconformists, FRASs will often break the rules of the game just for the fun or the thrill of it.

Popular Vocations

These high-energy wheeler-dealers are naturally great salesmen (and women), incorporating their street-smart savvy in the worlds of real estate, investments, and automobiles, as well as virtually any other industry that entails promoting. They have an uncanny ability to make the money they often so lavishly spend.

These people of action use facts adroitly and think quickly on their feet. Hardwired with energy-expending, flexible Q1 circuitry, FRASs are designed to be masterful negotiators.

They are especially gifted in sensing the motivations of others. While other designs may often be oblivious to the motives of those around them, the FRAS has an uncanny ability to pick up clues from body language and other signals given by a prospect. They can train their "hawk eyes" on their target, rarely looking away, as they continue to read the person until they can discover what the prospect is after.

Naturally charming and witty, the fun-loving FRAS can captivate a prospect, closing the sale with their special gift of persuasion. Though not people-oriented Empathetics, FRASs have a special knack for making their care and concern for each prospect readily evident.

Their natural expertise in using their hands leads to careers in which they can work with tools, including auto mechanic, dentistry, and, of course, construction, where their often strong physique can be incorporated, as well.

Well-Known FRAS Designs

The "material girl" pop star, **Madonna**, personified the FRAS design in many ways, as her unabashed flair had fans and critics alike often on the edge of their seats wondering what she might do next during a performance.

Though not natural "actors," the FRAS brings a down-to-earth, action-oriented flair to the big screen. **John Wayne**, **Clint Eastwood**, **Burt Reynolds**, **Sylvester Stallone**, and **Arnold Schwarzenegger** have all personified this over the years.

Ideally hardwired for the quarterback position in football, it is no surprise that some of the greatest of all time in the NFL have shared this design. **Johnny Unitas**, **Joe Namath**, **Joe Montana**, **Dan Marino**, **John Elway**, **Brett Favre**, and **Peyton Manning** are among the many renowned QBs found sharing this innate circuitry.

Performance Keys

The II-1 FRAS is a person of *action*, with no time to waste and little patience for those who do. Some things in life, however, take time to appreciate and to come to fruition. The hard-charging FRAS may find it beneficial to stop (or at least *slow down* a little) and "smell the roses." Taking some time to enjoy life's simple pleasures is good advice for all of us, but the high-energy FRAS may benefit in particular by taking it to heart.

Though normally focused on the moment at hand, the FRAS must consider the long-term impact of decisions made today. Not only will this encourage better decision-making, but it will provide time for introspection and contemplation.

As a Q1 design with a dominant Sensing function, the FRAS can easily be drawn to material things. It will be helpful to learn appreciation for saving as much as spending.

In relationships with others, the naturally street-smart FRAS may be prone to selfishness and manipulation. These tendencies can be overcome with active consideration of others by practicing faithfulness and tact. Learning to appreciate the value of humility will be beneficial for cultivating relationships.

II-2 BRAS — "Intense Artisan"

BACK, RIGHT-BRAIN (Q2), ANALYTIC, SENSATE
(deeply compares and appraises impersonal observations)
Order of Function Dominance: *ANALYTIC*, SENSING, Conceptual, empathetic

Appearance

The II-2 BRAS often appears quiet and reserved, especially to those who don't know them well. With a serious, stern demeanor, their natural "poker face" generally conceals what they may be thinking. Lacking any felt need to impress others, they tend to opt for simple outfits that are far from flamboyant. Unlike their Front-brained counterpart, the BRAS generally elects to go with more comfortable and economical attire.

The BRAS is relatively unconcerned with what others think, which includes what may be the prevailing fashion trends. BRAS females may tend to dress more masculine than most women, depending, of course, on how they were raised.

Not wordy by nature, the BRAS is characterized more by succinct, snappy speech. They may not feel compelled to communicate verbally, unless the topic involves something they consider to be of importance. When they are finally moved to speak, the BRAS may be distinguished by an inaudible mumble and speech that is often accompanied by a noticeable lisp.

BRAS designs may be more recognizable by their competitive natures. They are generally characterized as quiet, independent risk-takers. As dominant Analytics hardwired in posterior Q2, learning verbal skills may take a back seat to skill-oriented activities that require the use of tactical maneuvering. BRASs love working with their hands and are drawn to activities in which they can make use of tools.

Personality

Very serious about issues personally central to themselves, BRASs have little tolerance for the extraneous. They are often quick-tempered, due to an intensity that burns within.

As a dominant Analytic and secondary Sensate, the BRAS is very perceptive and seeks logical explanations in the quest to know why things are as they are. They may often deconstruct things in order to understand how they work. The BRAS has excellent spatial logic and is cunning in a "street smart" way. Shrewd and clever, the BRAS is impatient with logical inconsistency. Into the here-and-now, they eschew long-range planning, preferring to take action without delay.

Children

The young BRAS often appears quiet and reserved. Initially, it may be difficult for anyone other than their parents and siblings to understand their mumbling. This is especially true for BRAS boys, due to slower development of their left hemisphere.

The spoken language center, Broca's area, is located in Q3 (Front, Left). Accordingly, the four FL hardwired designs excel here. The opposite quadrant of the brain—Q2 (the Right posterior)—is the least communicative area, and it is here where the four BR designs are hardwired to excel, including the BRAS. It is, therefore, no surprise that learning to express themselves verbally is a challenge to the BRAS. They may require help pronouncing and enunciating their words. They need time and patience in order to open up and express their true thoughts.

Superseding the development of verbal skills is the desire for activities requiring skill and tactics. BRASs thrive on excitement and fast-moving adventure. As youngsters, they are fearless risk-takers, especially boys. Whether on top of a jungle gym, out on a diving board, or facing a hard-throwing pitcher, the courageous BRAS often amazes peers and parents with his or her bravado.

Though not natural conversationalists, they tend to win friends with their fraternal and optimistic disposition. BRASs generally limit their circle of friends to a small, close-knit group.

With a strong innate desire for freedom and autonomy, the BRAS can be strongly resistant to authority. This can lead to finding trouble that limits the freedom which they value so highly.

The BRAS has arguably the most academic potential of any of the eight hardwired Sensate designs. Many do poorly in school, however, due to lack of interest and self-discipline.

II-2 BRAS Traits

Appearance
- AS "hawk eyes," piercing look
- "poker face," serious and stern countenance
- clothing is trouble-free (what's comfy and cost-effective) without the felt need to impress others
- women dressing more masculine
- not ostentatious, unpretentious

Personality
- inner intensity, concise, short and snappy speech
- may speak with noticeable lisp, sometimes inaudible mumble
- witty, but usually not wordy
- independent
- little tolerance for the extraneous
- prefers *doing* rather than talking
- may not communicate vocally with others unless it involves something considered to be of importance
- often athletic, cunning
- very serious about issues personally central to self
- perceptive, keen and discerning
- shrewd, sly, clever
- fearless, daring and risk-taking
- machine and tool-oriented
- impatient with logical inconsistency
- often quick-tempered

Athletic Characteristics
- superior hand-eye coordination (fine-motor positioning)
- athletic, coordinated
- visually and tactically smart, thrive on "seizing the moment"
- "trained killer" in competition, tremendous desire to win
- offensive-minded with high aptitude for defense
- cunning, wily, deceptive
- plays by the rules unless it entails losing, at which point anything goes

Athletic Characteristics

Supremely designed for athletic competition, the intense BRAS combines superior hand-eye coordination with a cunning strategic mindset and a killer instinct. This Back-brained Analytic Sensate is able to block out distractions and focus on the goal like no other hardwired design.

The BRAS combines tactical intelligence with excellent situational awareness. Unlike most other designs, the BRAS is offensive-minded, yet possesses a naturally high defensive aptitude, as well. BRAS athletes have a tremendous desire to win, at virtually any cost.

BRASs are masters of logical deception. They are naturally skilled in setting up their opponent, as they feign one move, only to execute another. From waging battle in the professional ranks to a neighborhood pickup game, the BRAS plays to win.

At a young age, however, these Back-brained Analytics may become caught up in "thinking" issues, leading to awkwardness and uncertainty, as they play with seeming reckless abandon. Because their primary Analytic function trumps their secondary Sensing, the inexperienced BRAS may think first, and then react.

Interestingly, this Analytic dominance may lead to the adherence of superstitions, which is a characteristic of many BRAS athletes. MLB hall-of-famer **Wade Boggs** was known as the "Chicken Man" because of his pre-game fowl-eating ritual. Whenever possible, he also made it a point to take his pre-game batting practice at 5:17 p.m. and run his pre-game wind sprints at 7:17 p.m.

As with all Sensates, they are empirical learners, who will improve with experience. They love to get their hands (and whole body) dirty, competing as bold, hard-nosed daredevils on the field of play.

Practice is far from a bore to the BRAS, who views it as not only necessary, but fun. Known to train like no other design, hours go by like minutes for the BRAS athletes focused on refining their skill. With an innate desire for freedom, however, the intense and aggressive BRAS may run afoul of coaches who demand restrictive control. This may result in the misunderstood BRAS getting benched, suspended, or worse.

Popular Vocations

The action-oriented BRAS is a true craftsman, gifted in the use of their hands. They are drawn to virtually any activity that makes use of tools. From athletic equipment, to the artist's brush, to the carpenter's drill, to the surgeon's scalpel, tools provide this intense artisan a needed outlet for self-expression.

With relentless dedication to activities they enjoy, they normally excel in their craft, often at the expense of other priorities. Their superior spatial abilities provide outstanding artistic proficiency, as well as a distinct advantage in competitive athletics.

Drawn to jobs with practical applications in which they can make use of their hands, the BRAS can be found not only in athletics, but also construction, mechanics, machine operation, and sculpting. They can be master surgeons, as well, if they choose the medical profession.

While making long-term plans is not their strong suit, they are supreme tactical strategists, with a keen awareness of the here-and-now. The BRAS can find success in virtually any profession, due to an intense drive to master their area of interest. Prone to become fixated on whatever fascinates them, BRASs are known to put in long hours, often easily losing track of time. This may result in the BRAS neglecting important priorities. While this single-minded dedication contributes to success in the area of interest, it can also lead to problems in other areas of life.

Though their Back-brained hardwiring leads to deep reflection, the BRAS can often display what appears to be a seeming "extraverted" persona when in comfortable surroundings or when they feel especially competent in their vocation. In such a case, they will often become talkative and outspoken. Even then, their speech is straightforward and efficient, lacking extraneous adjectives and verbiage.

BRASs possess a great sense of timing, coupled with a knack for stark realism. Their cunning instincts can lead to interest and success in securities trading, finance, law enforcement and criminal investigation. They are also drawn to vocations that are accompanied by an element of danger, such as racing, aviation, and the military.

Well-Known BRAS Designs

Michael Jordan, **Larry Bird**, **Ty Cobb**, and **Pete Rose** are a few athletic superstars who have personified the intense drive of the BRAS. Not only were they known for their competitive fire, but their work ethic was legendary. **Jimmy Connors**, **John McEnroe**, and **Martina Navratilova** challenged the concept of tennis being a "gentleman's sport," as they competed with an outward intensity rarely seen before on the court.

Bobby Knight, **Mike Ditka**, and **Bill Cowher** are coaching examples of the BRAS intensity on the sideline. From the ice to the links, BRAS athletes have ranked among the top in their game. **Wayne Gretzky** and **Mario Lemeiux** dominated the NHL for years, while **Ben Hogan** and **Karrie Webb** stood atop the golfing world in their time, as well.

Performance Keys

As a dominant Analytic wired strongest in Q2, the II-2 BRAS is not naturally a "people" person. The natural intensity that serves this design so well on the athletic field can be detrimental when it comes to interpersonal relationships. It is important to seek a positive outlet for this intensity, as well as to give consideration to others' point of view when in disagreement.

It is typical of Right-brained Sensates to sacrifice planning for the future as they become caught up in the events of the moment, and the BRAS design is no different. Laying out a schedule, even if only for the upcoming week, can be a beneficial practice. Once the discipline is gained to stick to a weekly schedule, the transition to a more comprehensive monthly structure and longer can begin, as long-term targets are put into focus. The daily satisfaction in realizing the long-term consequences of today's decisions will be significant.

Finally, when it comes to potentially debilitating superstitions, the BRAS must understand that their excellent physical and mental skills do not require the burden of groundless notions.

II-3 FLAS — "Director"

FRONT, LEFT-BRAIN (Q3), ANALYTIC, SENSATE
(critiques, acts on, and communicates impersonal observations)
Order of Function Dominance: *ANALYTIC*, SENSING, Conceptual, empathetic

Appearance

The II-3 FLAS is born with hardwired supervisory tendencies. Well-groomed with good posture, they will not hesitate to give direction and orders, naturally gravitating to positions of leadership. Organized and tidy, the FLAS presents a picture of control in all that they do.

Brimming with confidence, the FLAS is alert to personal appearance. They will normally be found tastefully dressed in traditional attire. Animated speakers, they often incorporate energetic hand gestures into their speech. They make good eye contact with their piercing "hawk eyes."

Personality

The high-energy FLAS gives directives easily, with a practical, logic-based bent. They are born with an inherent need for control. Empathy is their innately weakest function, leaving them with a tendency to be matter-of-factly critical if they fail to parse their words carefully.

Capable supervisors, they are organized and efficient. The FLAS enjoys deciding what must be done and then implementing the procedures to get there. Managing a project to completion drives the FLAS, who cherishes the respect of peers and family for a job well done.

The FLAS leads with a single-minded determination that may prompt others to consider them heavy-handed dictators. With a precise thought process, the opinionated FLAS may be prone to prejudge others and situations. They are often short-tempered.

Normally serious-minded with a tradition-based mindset, FLASs take pride in being capable, persistent leaders. They are resistant to change, mainly due to the unknown that accompanies it, not the least of which is the possibility it could endanger their capacity to maintain control.

Because of their high standards for associates, they may have a tendency to withdraw to the pleasure of their own company. This desire for solitude may lead to a seeming Back-brained appearance, and FLASs, indeed, often view themselves that way. Do not be fooled. As is often the case, *energy level* is key. While persona may sometimes resemble that of the fellow Left-brained II-4 BLAS, the Front-brained FLAS has the greater energy and drive.

FLASs occupy many leadership positions. Some are considered warm, fun, witty, and great conversationalists, while others may be seen as cold, judgmental and controlling. These apparent wide-ranging personalities highlight the problem with conventional assessment methods. Donning the "mask" appropriate for the situation, the FLAS often demonstrates the mood they feel will best help them control a given situation. If they believe the tough side is necessary, you will most likely be treated sternly. Conversely, if they believe a persuasive approach is best for the moment, you will find yourself being charmed.

One other notable characteristic of the FLAS is when they "extravert" in the Front of the brain, they engage their dominant Analytic "thinking" function. When they do this, their critical eye for right and wrong is active, leading them to criticize freely and matter-of-factly. When they want or need to get along with others, however, they will make it a point to temper their opinions.

Children

The naturally responsible FLAS child takes charge effortlessly, getting things done with ease. They have a tendency to be bossy, often oblivious to the feelings of their peers. As dominant Analytics, hardwired in the Front brain, they feely express their logical "thinking" function.

FLAS children respect authorities who are organized and decisive. They appreciate precise instructions and want to know what is expected of them. The enjoy subjects that are structured and practical.

These high-energy Sensates can be high achievers in school, especially when they can implement experimentation, observation, and other hands-on methods. Memorizing facts comes easier than

II-3 FLAS Traits

Appearance
- traditional in attire
- vibrant, gesticulates
- dresses in traditional fashion with taste
- organized, tidy, appears in control
- good posture, well groomed
- AS "hawk eyes"
- very confident looking, alert to personal appearance
- gives eye contact

Personality
- usually serious minded
- efficient, industrious, precise
- critical, leader
- traditional
- pragmatic, hardheaded, matter-of-fact, no-nonsense, realistic
- energetic, driven
- persistent, single-minded, determined, taskmaster
- opinionated, prone to prejudge
- domineering, bossy, capable, supervisor
- organized, administrative
- may be dictatorial, heavy-handed
- often short-tempered

Athletic Characteristics
- superior fine-motor dexterity
- king of hustle
- injury prone
- mechanical, tight or stiff unless well-developed in sports
- prone to hurting others (by accident or purposely)
- defensive-minded
- good with logistics
- plays by rules but often may deliver "cheap shot" as result of competitive nature

dealing with abstract concepts. Organized and responsible, the FLAS desires to know in advance when the assignment is due, thus providing time to plan for its completion.

Naturally resistant to change, the young FLAS may display a quick temper when unable to control the situation. This insecurity may cause a lack of confidence, as FLASs have an inborn fear of failure.

Ideas for FLASs are only as good as how well they can be applied. To speculate or merely discuss theory is a waste of time to the highly efficient and pragmatic FLAS. Ideas must work in order to be valued by this highly pragmatic design.

FLASs tend to choose practical college majors and vocations that are necessary for the everyday functioning of society. They are frequently found pursuing degrees and careers in a business-oriented field.

Athletic Characteristics

Possessing superior fine-motor dexterity, FLASs can be good athletes. Their Front-brained energy and Left-brained deliberateness, however, can often give them a bull-in-a-china-shop appearance on the athletic field. They may appear tight or stiff unless they have carefully developed their skills.

Kings of hustle, FLASs charge ahead with determination and confidence, often leading to injury, both to their opponents, as well as themselves. As they mature, they gain a better ability to control their often tense, high-energy approach. This shows itself in more polished motor movements with less tension in the wrist and hand (fine-motor) area. The more they can relax this inherent fine-motor tension under pressure, the better they will be able to perform.

Defensive-minded and good with logistics, FLASs naturally gravitate toward coaching, even while still active participants. With an innate desire to control the action, coaching provides an ideal conduit.

FLASs play by the rules, but may be known to deliver a "cheap shot" as a result of their competitive nature.

Popular Vocations

Strong-willed and decisive, the FLAS is specially designed with a knack for setting goals and pushing to reach them. Gifted in administration, organization, and presiding over activities, they have a natural aptitude for business. Naturally compelled to ensure things are handled properly, FLASs are inclined to incorporate rules and regulations.

They are often considered "workaholics," known by their tireless dedication to getting the job done. Rarely can a FLAS be found who is considered lazy on the job, as they are naturally driven to work their way to the top of their field.

Resistant to change, the tradition-minded FLAS is inclined to maintain the status quo, which can lead to being perceived as controlling and inflexible. They give directives easily, often oblivious to the needs and feelings of others.

The FLAS can frequently be found in vocations involving the tangible—facts, money, and objects. Management, banking, finance, accounting, commerce, law, and secretarial work are all frequent destinations in the business world. Teaching and coaching are natural fits, as well. They are also drawn to politics, education administration, home economics, law enforcement, and even cosmetology. Of course, the military is a perfect match for their innate desire for order and discipline.

Well-Known FLAS Designs

Gerald Ford, **Richard Nixon**, and **Bob Dole** are a few well-known FLAS names of recent years in the political realm. It should be no surprise that legendary basketball coach **Dean Smith** was the one who popularized use of the four-corners "stall" offense. What better way to *control* the action! The NFL's **Mike Holmgren** and **George Allen** represent two more high-energy FLAS coaching minds.

On the pitching mound, hall-of-fame flamethrower **Nolan Ryan** exemplified the hard-charging power of the FLAS. Ryan was known not only for his blazing fastball, but also for his strong work ethic.

Legendary PGA golfer **Nick Faldo** was another top performer renowned for his intimidating presence, intense work ethic, and single-minded dedication to his game.

Performance Keys

As a dominant Analytic wired strongest in Q3, the II-3 FLAS has a naturally predominant attention to detail and adherence to rules. This may lead to being overly critical with those who fail to follow procedure. It is beneficial to remember that when it comes to dealing with people, no one is perfect—including the FLAS.

In order to be the most effective leader, the FLAS should encourage others by consciously expressing praise and good feelings. There is no better place to start this than in the home, where comfort with family can easily lead to frequent critiques. Being cognizant of incorporating tact with the truth in their words will go a long way toward softening the often gruff communication style of the FLAS.

A distinct trait of this Left-brained, Analytic, Sensing mind is the intense drive to accomplish the goal ahead. While this can be beneficial, it can also often be accompanied by tunnel vision that prevents the FLAS from spotting other opportunities or making beneficial adjustments along the way. Eliciting input from a Conceptual can help to bring balance to the perspective of the FLAS. Learning to listen with an open mind and to appreciate the opinions of others will prove beneficial.

Finally, making it a point to take a periodic break will not only re-energize this driven design, but will provide helpful perspective for dealing with others who are hardwired differently.

II-4 BLAS — "Perfectionist Inspector"

BACK, LEFT-BRAIN (Q4), ANALYTIC, SENSATE
(methodically classifies observations impersonally)

Order of Function Dominance: *SENSING*, ANALYTIC, Empathetic, conceptual

Appearance

The II-4 BLAS almost always possesses a slight, thin build. In fact, if you find an overweight BLAS, chances are high that you have assessed him or her incorrectly. BLASs generally possess the most slender build of all sixteen hardwired designs.

Their dominant Sensing function combined with Back, Left-brained (Q4) wiring provides them with the most discerning sense of when they are full. Though they may enjoy the occasional sweet tooth, they are the least apt of all designs to overeat. Also, as energy-conserving Back-brainers, they generally require less food than energy-expending Front-brainers.

Usually neat and conventionally dressed in ordinary, quiet colors, the BLAS features a conservative smile to match their normal attire. Overall, they are discreet and orderly. Men often have straight hair, usually with a short, conservative cut.

With a modest appearance and demeanor, the BLAS features a look of seriousness, including their natural "hawk eyes." They speak in a careful, deliberate manner with a quiet and somewhat monotone voice.

Personality

Reserved and quiet by nature, the BLAS is stiffly dignified. This private person would never be characterized as a loose, free spirit. BLASs are helpful, cooperative and kind, though not necessarily warm-hearted. They favor discipline over compassion.

Sensitive to their surroundings to the point of distraction, the BLAS is overly aware of minutiae. Temperature, odors, sounds, and sights preoccupy their conscious and subconscious minds. Guarded and cautious, this Sensing awareness can be debilitating if unchecked. They are alert and attentive, desiring to tend to matters themselves, as opposed to delegating. They are logical and thorough with a compelling desire to bring order to everything they can.

Though aloof and artless, this straightforward design is steady and dependable. They say what they mean and mean what they say. The conservative BLAS is reticent to try new things, preferring the certainty of the here-and-now over what may develop from stepping out into the unknown.

The BLAS is hard-working and dependable. Even free time must have a purpose and be task-oriented. Though an innately reluctant leader, the BLAS may be given a position of authority, due to their organized and efficient nature. At ease with logic and words, the BLAS may appear to have an outgoing nature, but is, in fact, one of the most private of the hardwired designs.

Children

Naturally organized and dutiful, BLAS children are generally easy to raise. They are at ease with family rules and routine, secure with the order and control therein. As Back-brained Analytics, they value time alone for reflection.

BLASs have a keen interest in the physical world around them. With their Left-brained tunnel vision, they can become single-focused on their area of interest, going into far deeper detail than most other hardwired designs would care to venture.

Though they will dig deep into a subject or topic of interest, their naturally lower Back-brained energy level may lead them to cut short the study of subjects in which the fascination is lacking. In particular, they are generally not drawn to abstract, theoretical subjects, instead favoring more practical matters that can be more easily quantified. As such, they may easily become bogged down in ancillary details, often needing help to grasp the big picture.

When it comes to their studies, the BLAS requires a quiet, organized setting more than most. Their dominant Sensing Left brain is easily distracted by surrounding noise or activity. BLASs build their knowledge base and form their positions on issues by accumulating mountains of relevant data. They are not prone to pull a position on a topic out of "thin air" and will be highly unlikely to register a viewpoint until they have accumulated sufficient evidence to support their stance.

II-4 BLAS Traits

Appearance
- AS "hawk eyes"
- generally thin and slight
- neatly and conventionally dressed
- ordinary to quiet colors in clothing
- discreet, orderly, men often have straight hair (short)
- conservative smile, serious look
- modest
- deliberate and careful speech

Personality
- solitary, reserved, private, quiet
- more stiffly dignified than loosely free-spirited
- kind (not necessarily warm), helpful, cooperative
- steady, reliable, dependable, stable, conservative
- sensitive to surroundings, very aware of minutiae
- immovable, straightforward, artless
- aloof, guarded, cautious
- alert and attentive
- logical, thorough, compelled to bring order to matters

Athletic Characteristics
- superior fine-motor dexterity
- stiff but fundamentally sound mechanics
- lower energy
- injury-prone
- defensive-minded
- team player
- good with logistics
- plays well within the rules and appreciates the rules

Athletic Characteristics

As Q4 Sensing Analytics, the BLAS relies heavily on the Left brain, naturally processing matters sequentially. With an innate desire to see things done properly and with control, the BLAS naturally takes a conservative, defensive approach to sport. When their confidence and motivation levels are high, however, they can become aggressive, with the potential for extraordinary concentration and focus.

They have stiff, but fundamentally sound mechanics, featuring superior fine-motor dexterity. Like all Left-brainers, they may be more injury-prone, despite operating at a generally lower energy level than their Front-brained counterparts.

It often takes an important event for BLASs to give full effort, particularly in an offensive mode. When the big event involves a team sport, BLASs want to make sure they contribute their share. They are naturally inclined to give extra effort for the team's sake.

They are good team players, more than willing to allow the spotlight to shine on teammates. They also do well with logistics, appreciating the preciseness of the game plan.

The BLAS not only plays within the rules, but appreciates having them in place. They are not ones to showboat or talk trash, and are generally liked and respected by both teammates and opponents.

Popular Vocations

Organized and structured, these trustworthy perfectionists excel in hands-on, practical occupations. They enjoy using their strong Analytic function for logical problem-solving, and will use painstaking care in addressing even the smallest detail.

Supervising work that requires detailed scrutiny is a natural fit for the meticulous BLAS. While not as controlling as their Front-brained counterparts, BLASs respect leadership and expect others to do the same. They value rules and strive to maintain order in all they do.

The BLAS is a natural fit in the business world, filling roles in accounting and bookkeeping, law, banking, tax examining, financial planning, insurance, and secretarial work. They do not prefer the world of sales. Though BLASs can be capable and convincing, their Back-brained hardwiring can be an obstacle for selling. If in sales, they greatly prefer to service the long-time customer over cold calling.

They can also be found in engineering, computer programming, and the physical sciences, in addition to law enforcement, military, fire fighting and farming.

Well-Known BLAS Designs

Coaching is another profession in which the relatively rare BLAS can be found. Not only do they appreciate the discipline that accompanies a well-run team, but they have an innate desire to perfect the combination of Xs and Os in their meticulous game planning. Basketball's legendary **John Wooden** and **Mike Krzyzewski**, as well as NFL Hall of Famer **Tom Landry** all exemplify the dignified BLAS.

Golfing legend **Jack Nicklaus** and **Chris Evert** of tennis fame also shared the BLAS hardwiring. On the baseball diamond, **Orel Hershiser** personified the thinking-man's pitcher.

Performance Keys

As a dominant Sensate wired strongest in the Back, Left quadrant (Q4), the II-4 BLAS has an inherent tendency to obsess over the details of the moment. While this can be helpful when it comes to ensuring all the "T"s are crossed and "I"s are dotted, it can also result in difficulty seeing the big picture. Taken to an extreme, the continual awareness of relative minutiae can become a debilitating distraction.

The solitary disposition of this painstaking design can often leave the BLAS aloof to the needs of others. By making it a point to express praise, appreciation, and affirmation when the opportunity arises, the BLAS can cultivate healthy relationships. Building friendships outside of the business world will be beneficial, as well. Though the BLAS can become quite firm in held convictions, it is important to be open to the input of others.

One more area of concern is the tendency to become obsessed with a particular area of interest, be it business or hobby. Making it a point to plan recreation times with others, as well as alone, can be a healthy practice.

Perhaps the best advice for the persnickety BLAS is to learn to let the little things slide. Life is too short to constantly sweat the small stuff!

NOTE: Despite being one of the least common designs, an inordinately high number of people tend to view themselves as possessing the relatively rare hardwired circuitry of the BLAS. On commercial personality inventories, as well as informal self-assessments, the BLAS equivalent is among the most common results, while in reality, it is quite the opposite. Men in particular seem to place a high value on the reserved, pragmatic, logical, and organized traits of the "Perfectionist Inspector." Understanding hardwired designs, especially the body skill traits, quickly reveals the true BLAS, which is actually among the least commonly found designs in the U.S.

11
Region
III
Empathetic Conceptuals

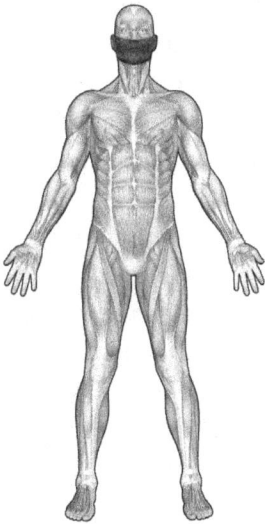

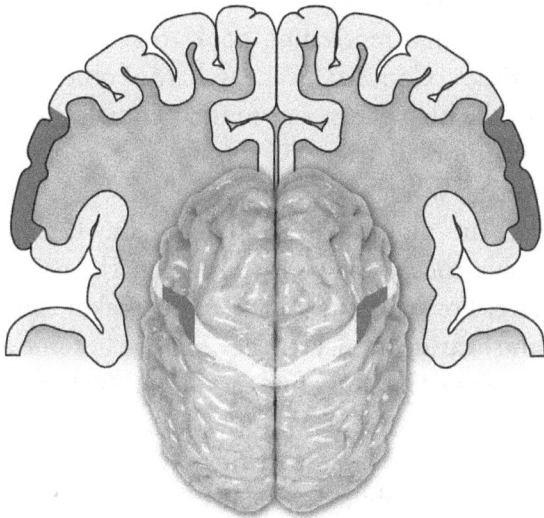

EC **Body Skill Group**

IMAGINE **PERSONALLY**

Region III - Empathetic Conceptuals
Mouth Region Skilled

Empathetic Concepuals tend to value integrity and encourage others to seek it, as well. They have a strong desire to communicate, often through various forms of media. For this reason, ECs are often found in teaching, acting, writing, preaching, and professional communications media (TV, radio, journalism, etc.). ECs believe the best about others and value relationships. Devoted to friends, family and their vocations, they tend to be romantic and visionary. ECs are often optimistic about future possibilities.

Personal Imaginers tend to see potential good in nearly everything. They may be easily associated with the possibility thinking found in success and motivation books that urge readers to adopt a positive attitude. Concern for the welfare of others marks the EC, accounting for the high percentage found in nursing and missionary work. With a flair for language, EC communicators excel in both the written and spoken word.

The motor skill strength of the Personal Imaginers is further down the motor cortex in region III, providing proficiency in the face, lips, jaw, and tongue. This makes the EC a language, speech, and hearing specialist. They can also become excellent at coordinating gross-motor and fine-motor movements with body flexibility (especially RECs). Because they are dominant in neither the gross or fine motors, yet hardwired in close proximity to both, ECs appear to have the ability to readily gain coordination of both. Empathetic Conceptuals—particularly Right-brainers—can be among the most graceful acrobats.

III-1 FREC — "Motivational Dynamo"

FRONT, RIGHT-BRAIN (Q1), EMPATHETIC, CONCEPTUAL
(quickly explores and responds to imaginations personally)

Order of Function Dominance: *CONCEPTUAL*, EMPATHETIC, Analytic, sensing

Appearance

The III-1 FREC is an outgoing, high-energy Front-brainer, which shows through in a bright, warm appearance, normally adorned in colorful attire. With a strong innate desire for self-expression, FRECs will often showcase their individuality in the form of expressive dress.

The FREC is generally characterized by a bright countenance with a loose, uninhibited smile and a wide-eyed look. The hair of FRECs may be curly more often than that of most other designs. Masculine characteristics of males may be less pronounced than with that of other hardwired designs, as well. This may even be seen in the FREC's gait, which is smooth, yet may have an emphasis of walking a bit up on their toes.

FRECs are generally quick-speaking people with a wide range of voice inflection. They are frequently characterized by their distinctive, funny, and infectious laugh.

Personality

The dynamic FREC exudes enthusiasm and brings fun to even the most routine tasks. Charismatic and highly verbal, this friendly "extraverting" Front-brained design is a born cheerleader, naturally encouraging others to be their best. They see each day dawning with new possibilities, actively recruiting others to join them with their infectious enthusiasm.

With a highly active imagination, the FRAC energetically bounces from one activity to the next, creating even more energy, and naturally inspiring others to come along. There is rarely a dull moment in the presence of these inspirational dynamos.

Social and charismatic, FRECs generously give affection, time, and energy to everyone around them. Naturally going to great lengths in an effort to help others, the FREC may keep going until exhaustion hits. FRECs value the appreciation normally elicited by their assistance, and can be very sensitive to criticism.

Emotionally driven, they tend to wear their heart on their sleeve. Few can match the outgoing warmth and affirmation of the FREC.

As Right-brained Conceptuals, they conduct their lives with an easy flexibility in their schedule. Because they are dominant Conceptuals, however, as well as people-oriented Empathetics, this inherently flexible and dreamy nature can lead to them being somewhat flighty and scatterbrained.

Children

FREC children are captivating and fun to be around. They have an uncanny ability to charm their way out of the trouble where their impulsive, seat-of-the-pants nature so often leads. FRECs march to the beat of their own drum, detesting the constricting nature of a structured schedule.

Social and charismatic, FRECs give freely of themselves, lavishing affection on all those around them. They idealize relationships, and are frequently chosen for positions of leadership, as others admire their energetic ideas and skills of persuasion.

FRECs enjoy reading, as they envision the possibilities of the future in their fertile minds. They can easily become immersed in projects that arouse their passion, yet just as quickly see that curiosity wane, as new stimuli piques their interest. While they take joy in planning for the future, those visions can seemingly change with the wind in their younger years.

With copious amounts of natural energy, FRECs look for variety and action in their daily lives. Structured classroom environments with their monotonous routine often leave the FREC student feeling confined and restricted. FRECs are often musically inclined, and can be found playing a variety of instruments.

FREC children thrive by being around others, doing well with group projects. They often need help with structure and meeting deadlines, however, as their dominant Conceptual mind may often lead them to lose awareness of time.

Athletic Characteristics

Due to the Empathetic Conceptual's region III location on the primary motor cortex, it appears they are able to coordinate the fine

III-1 FREC Traits

Appearance
- dresses colorfully and expressively
- bright and warm appearance , unashamed to be different
- may walk on toes, smooth gait
- may have curly hair
- masculine characteristics sometimes less pronounced in males
- often wide-eyed, loose, uninhibited smile with a bright countenance

Personality
- friendly, enthusiastic, zesty
- easy flexibility in schedule
- highly verbal
- speaks quickly with wide range of voice inflection
- cheerful, bubbly, vivacious, animated, "full of life"
- supportive
- theatrical, dramatic, over-the-top, exaggerated
- having fun in everyday tasks
- charismatic
- scatterbrained, flighty

Athletic Characteristics
- coordinate fine and gross-motor muscle movements with fluidity
- graceful, acrobatic, leaper
- extremely high energy
- often explosive
- nimble, agile, very supple
- spur-of-the-moment
- natural, offensive minded
- good endurance, very high pain threshold in competition
- play by the rules but may test the boundaries

and gross-motor movements quite naturally. Combined with the Q1 dominance of the FREC, we find a highly energetic, fluid acrobat. Not only are these Right-brained Conceptuals nimble and agile, but they are graceful, as well. It follows, based on their innate tendency to incorporate their toes a bit more in their gait, that they are explosive leapers.

Participating with a high degree of energy, these spontaneous, offensive-minded acrobats operate with creative ingenuity. When performing before a big audience, such as during the Olympic Games, the adrenaline rush is often so great that FRECs usually forget the difficulty of their routines and engage them with uncharacteristic boldness. This may lead them to accomplish feats they may not have even thought possible.

FRECs are emotional competitors. Their strong Empathetic function combined with their high-energy Q1 circuitry provide them with passionate energy, which they feed off. Even when not in the game, these natural cheerleaders can be found energetically encouraging and rooting on their teammates from the sideline. FREC **M.L. Carr**, a reserve player on the great Boston Celtics teams of the early 1980s, was frequently featured on television broadcasts enthusiastically waving a towel in support of his teammates.

Another area of athletic competition in which FRECs excel is they have arguably the highest pain threshold. As dominant Conceptuals hardwired in the Front brain, the naturally weakest function of the FREC is Back-brained Sensing—the function most in touch with physical pain. When engaged in athletic competition, the high-energy Q1 FRECs kick their Conceptual function into high gear, channeling their mental and physical energies with amazing focus.

They are also highly adept at visualizing, as their dominant and spatial Right-brained Conceptual function is used to imagine multi-dimensional events in their lives. FRECs regularly incorporate this ability to build confidence, perfect their technique, and activate regions of the brain important for athletic success.

On a sidenote, FRECs can be excellent jugglers, along with the fellow Q1 Conceptual FRAC. The dominant Conceptual function enables the mind to visualize where the object will be, combined with the Q1 circuitry that provides great spatial awareness, along with the speed for the hands and mind to keep up with the flying objects.

Popular Vocations

Naturally optimistic, FRECs are supreme "possibility thinkers," often energizing the workplace with their contagious enthusiasm. Though generally able to work well with others, the vivacious FREC possesses an independent spirit, especially when it comes to rules and regulations. They need freedom to explore their vision, though their strong personal values and desire to please generally lead to them being good team players.

FRECs are enthusiastic sales people who excel in closing the deal. Both in person, as well as on the telephone, they speak with a warm, comfortable tone, providing an incomparable optimistic, personal touch. As team and organization leaders, they take charge with infectious enthusiasm and vision. FRECs work best with people and ideas, leaving the monotonous administrative details to others.

The entrepreneurial FREC cherishes the latitude to follow a dream and will be drawn to careers such as music, acting, and entertaining. Their creative mind also leads them to play and screen writing, journalism, advertising, and public relations.

Because FRECs naturally enjoy helping and encouraging others, meaningful service-oriented careers are another realm in which they can be found. These may include roles in the ministry, counseling, psychology, human services, and other health-related professions. One thing is certain, no matter the career, the FREC will be found working with energy and passion.

Well-Known FREC Designs

Oprah Winfrey rose from poverty in rural Mississippi to become an entertainment icon. With genuine warmth, Oprah combined plainspoken curiosity and robust humor to become the most popular talk show host on television. She is adored and appreciated in large part because of her natural encouragement and compassion for her guests, as well as her audience.

Comedian **Bob Hope** also shared the infectious FREC wiring, which drove him to carry his popular act around the world, entertaining and boosting the morale of active service American military personnel. Other FRECs in the world of entertainment include **Ted Danson** and **Goldie Hawn**.

Olympic champion figure skater **Kristi Yamaguchi** exemplified the graceful, energetic FREC on the ice, while NFL Hall of Fame wide receiver **Jerry Rice** showcased his explosive acrobatics on the gridiron.

The music world has featured such FRECs as **Whitney Houston**, **Diana Ross**, **Reba McEntire**, **Amy Grant**, and **Barbara Mandrell**. Mandrell personified the FREC, as the multi-talented instrumentalist played the accordion, bass guitar, banjo, guitar, mandolin, pedal steel guitar, dobro, and saxophone, often switching between instruments in the midst of the same number!

Performance Keys

While the energetic passion of the III-1 FREC can often be a positive, it may also lead to pushing forward with action before fully thinking through the situation. Practicing the self-discipline of stepping back and considering all the facts may help to avoid reliance on improvising too often. Ensuring that observations are grounded in reality will help to successfully reach the visionary goals that drive this motivated design.

There is one important caveat for the FREC when it comes to visionary thinking. It is important to separate dreams from what is most likely to occur. With advance consideration of both possibilities and probabilities, appropriate logic can be better incorporated.

One of the best attributes of the FREC is their infectious enthusiasm. Just as they thrive on this energy, it can be especially effective when they also use it to help motivate and encourage those around them. Perhaps most importantly, FRECs must be aware of their passionate tendencies as they encounter life's highs and lows, lest they fall victim to riding an emotional roller coaster.

III-2 BREC — "Imaginative Romantic"

BACK, RIGHT-BRAIN (Q2), EMPATHETIC, CONCEPTUAL
(deeply compares and appraises personal imaginations)

Order of Function Dominance: *EMPATHETIC*, CONCEPTUAL, Sensing, analytic

Appearance

The III-2 BREC often presents a reticent, shy demeanor. BRECs are normally good listeners with a warm smile, yet struggle to make eye contact. They generally speak softly. Their words tend to be deliberate, though sometimes may have a poetic feel.

Far from flashy in behavior or appearance, BRECs prefer comfort over fashion, normally opting for casual attire. Similar to the closely related Front-brained fellow REC, BRECs will often feature curly hair and may be characterized by a gait up on their toes.

Personality

Approachable and unassuming, the dominant Empathetic BREC has a good awareness of the feelings and needs of others. Though possessing a fertile, creative mind, BRECs may keep their thoughts to themselves, careful not to "rock the boat." Their strong values may be left unexpressed, at least until violated by others, at which point they may become emotional and demanding. BRECs value and strive for harmony in life.

As freedom-loving people, their powerful imaginations often lead them to a childlike, idealistic view of the world. Though often impractical, BRECs are not without special talents, by any means. They are creative romantics with powerful poetic literary skills.

Naturally timid and unsure of themselves, the sensitive BREC may be melancholy and unmotivated. With encouragement, however, their personable, friendly nature can show through. Often only family and close friends are able to get to know the considerate, humble BREC.

Children

BREC children are quintessential daydreamers, creating a fantasy world in which they may often mentally reside. Even as adults, this dream world can be difficult to leave behind, especially when feeling life's pressures. In an imperfect and ever-changing world, all too often marked by turmoil and chaos, BRECs often wish they could return to the innocence of their youth, similar to Peter Pan and Never Land—the place where children never grow up!

BRECs often find it difficult to express their own needs, as they strive to please teachers and parents. With thoughtful, delicate consciences, they require frequent positive reinforcement.

Poetic and philosophical, BRECs may not be particularly practical as they are idealistically driven to make a better world. The foremost question they carry with them through life is, "Who am I?"

As with all Empathetic Conceptuals, BRECs love learning about people. They like to consider the potential in others, as well as learn how others have maximized their abilities.

BRECs naturally attach emotion to virtually everything they encounter. Whether reading, writing, or thinking about others, these Right-brained, dominant Empathetics view issues from a personal standpoint. As Conceptuals, BRECs idealize the possibilities in people, and have a strong interest in personal development.

Athletic Characteristics

Similar to the closely related FREC, the BREC is a graceful, acrobatic athlete, featuring supreme fluid coordination of the big and small muscles. Sleek and agile, the BREC plays with finesse more than brute power, avoiding physical contact whenever possible.

BRECs are content to be more of a follower and rarely gravitate to leadership roles in team sports. They are also generally not argumentative. When things don't go their way, they are more likely to back down than put up a fight, especially if it would cause hard feelings.

BRECs are not naturally aggressive, particularly at the outset of competition. Unlike the four dominant Analytic designs, who may easily set out to "annihilate" their opponent from the start, the dominant Empathetics are not inclined to manufacture arbitrary "ill will" toward a fellow competitor.

With regard to athletic confidence, BRECs are similar to the I-2 BRES. As Q2 Empathetics, both are naturally inclined to view their mistakes more negatively and subjectively than most other hardwired

III-2 BREC Traits

Appearance
- comfortably and casually dressed
- soft deliberate (even poetic) speech
- struggles with eye contact
- warm smile
- often have curly hair
- good listener
- may walk on toes
- Rarely overweight

Personality
- unconventional, flexible
- approachable, unassuming, unimposing
- freedom-loving
- romantic
- melancholy
- supreme idealist, child-like at times
- timid, shy, often unsure of self
- may be unmotivated
- giving
- creative and imaginative, poetic, literary
- personable, friendly, considerate, sensitive, humble
- may be impractical

Athletic Characteristics
- fluid coordination of fine and gross-motor movements
- graceful, a "natural"
- may be quick
- sleek, agile
- limber, pliable, flexible
- plays with finesse, offensive primarily
- not argumentative, more of a follower than a leader
- not one to seek physical contact
- plays by the rules but may quit and/or shed a tear if not winning

designs. A tough-minded Analytic coach may easily magnify this issue. As BRECs normally perform according to how they feel, it is vital that they receive healthy doses of positive reinforcement from coaches, parents, and teammates. While anger, threats, and intimidation are questionable "motivation" techniques with most players, they are particularly destined to fail with the sensitive BREC.

Popular Vocations

BRECs are drawn to work that incorporates their strong personal values. They enjoy incorporating their beliefs in a way that helps others live to their full potential. Though hesitant to lead, BRECs bring creative ideas and make sensitive contributions to group dynamics.

BRECs may be found in psychology, psychiatry, medicine, science, ministry and missionary work. They enjoy teaching, as well, mainly English or Literature, utilizing their secondary Conceptual function to help students visualize their dreams. While more common at the higher grade levels, BRECs can sometimes be found in the more blithe atmosphere of Kindergarten, as well.

With a natural giftedness for writing, BRECs can also be found penning music, poetry, and other melodious prose. They are generally musically inclined, whether performing vocally, playing an instrument, or composing the music itself. Music provides comfort and recreation for the melancholy-prone BREC after a difficult day or in times of stress.

With a love of learning, BRECs willingly engage in the necessary training or continuing education to perform their job. They have a natural aversion to routine jobs, which is why writing makes for a good outlet for their creative Conceptual mind.

BRECs start many projects, but sometimes need encouragement and prodding to see them through to completion. Naturally flexible and adaptable, they may become easily distracted by surrounding activity, as they become overly idealistic in their relationships and disorganized in their work.

Well-Known BREC Designs

Naturally gifted with silky smooth coordination, most well-known BRECs are unsurprisingly found in the world of sports. NBA Hall of Famers **Julius ("Doctor J") Erving** and **Kareem Abdul-Jabbar** exemplified this smooth BREC fluidity on the hardwood. Seven-foot center **Dirk Nowitzki** is known as one of the NBA's smoothest shooting big men.

MLB Hall of Famer **Rod Carew** was known for his sweet swing, and New York Yankees legend **Derek Jeter** starred with his sleek, polished play.

Right-brainers have excellent spatial awareness, allowing them to replicate the movements of others. Conceptual Right-brainers often inject their own creativity, accordingly. The thoughtful Back-brained BREC is adept at illustrating what they see in this way. BREC **Tiger Woods** famously started down the road to stardom by mimicking his father's golf swing as a toddler.

As much as any hardwired design, the BREC can be especially impacted by their upbringing and "nurturing" environment. This factor is important to keep in mind when considering that Tiger Woods shares the same innate wiring as legendary pop icon, **Michael Jackson**. While both were raised by stern, demanding fathers, Tiger was molded into the world of competitive golf, where his imagination was filled only with creative golf shots and the vision of championships. Michael, by contrast, was ingrained in the world of music and entertainment, where his childlike dreaming was never really forced to grow up.

Both Tiger and Michael continued to strive for a virtually unreachable nirvana that led to their eventual undoing. Tiger, of course, had his notorious secret unquenchable lust for women, while Michael had the peculiar desire to constantly be surrounded by children (alone) at his extravagant estate. Michael even showed his childlike imagination in the naming of his estate, *Neverland* Ranch! Recall, also, how Michael could never find contentment in his outward appearance. Despite riches and superstardom, the pop icon was obsessed with a never-ending quest for the (unobtainable) "perfect" look, undergoing countless surgical cosmetic procedures.

Performance Keys

As a Q2 Empathetic Conceptual, the III-2 BREC is a quixotic visionary, often romanticizing the possibilities of tomorrow at the expense of overlooking the realities of today. This may lead to procrastination, particularly with projects that are not enjoyable. The end result can be falling into despair when obligations are not met.

The best remedy for this debilitating tendency is organization, which does not come naturally to the BREC. (The BREC, incidentally, is the opposite of arguably the most innately organized hardwired design, the II-3 FLAS.) Setting concrete short-term goals and being accountable to follow through with them will provide great benefit.

All hardwired designs must not forget that life is seldom ideal. Often their own toughest critic, BRECs may have a tendency to view their skills and accomplishments as insufficient, leaving them vulnerable to depression. We are best served maintaining practicality, accepting life as it comes and appreciating the joys of today, as opposed to longing for the "perfect" tomorrow that may never arrive.

Finally, the Back-brained BREC will benefit by overcoming their natural timidity to initiate new relationships and share their vivid imagination with others. This practice will help to avoid the innate tendency toward melancholy, instead promoting a joyful spirit within.

III-3 FLEC — "Enthusiastic Teacher"

Front, Left-brain (Q3), Empathetic, Conceptual
(critiques, acts on, and communicates personal imaginations)

Order of Function Dominance: *EMPATHETIC*, CONCEPTUAL, Sensing, analytic

Appearance

The demure III-3 FLEC generally presents in an attractive manner, tastefully and appropriately dressed for the occasion. With a warm, feeling smile, the intelligent-looking FLEC possesses an innate sense of style.

As one of the more reserved Front-brained designs, the FLEC features an even-tempered, graceful demeanor. Generally attractive and well-groomed, FLECs are seldom overweight. They can often be detected by the great care they give their appearance, though this can also lead to them being mistaken as a Sensing design.

Females strive to be thin, contemporary, fashionable, well-coiffed, and beautiful. Males take pride in being attractive, suave, and alluring.

Personality

Socially sophisticated, the naturally charming FLEC moves about with a graceful demeanor. Refined and well-mannered, FLECs are natural leading ladies and gentlemen. They are gifted in persuasive speech.

Generally low-key, as Front-brainers go, FLECs may not appear particularly outgoing on a one-to-one basis. Given leadership and an audience, however, the FLEC can develop into an expressive communicator.

FLECs are capable, if reluctant leaders. They do not take the lead by force, but when entrusted with a leadership position, they charismatically communicate their visions with fluent language skills, motivating others to follow.

With a strong Empathetic and considerate mindset, the FLEC is always willing and looking to help. This may lead to them unwittingly baring the hurts of others upon their own back. It can sometimes be a struggle for FLECs to keep their emotions under control, leaving them vulnerable to depression at times.

Cooperation and harmony are valued by FLECs, who consider personal relationships to be of great importance. They are idealistic when it comes to love and friendship, and can become disillusioned with a less than perfect mate or friend. Nonetheless, FLECs generally strive to look for the positive and hopeful side of life.

Children

FLEC children are warm and friendly, with a natural feel for relating to fellow children, as well as adults. They are generally responsible and well-behaved, obedient to rules and authority figures.

With a wide variety of interests, including athletics, drama, music, art, history, and literature, FLECs put a great deal of energy into doing them well.

They initiate friendships, seeking to build upon the natural goodness in others. FLECs have a strong need to be loved, which they inspire from others by possessing an innate sense of others' needs.

As Q3 designs (the human executive control center), FLECs are hardwired to be skilled with the inferior orbital left prefrontal cortex, which is the region of the brain associated with diplomatic, tactful, and winsome speech. Not only does this give all of the Q3 designs a strong propensity for structure, organization, and drive, but it provides FLECs in particular the ability to produce the right words to say in a friendly, positive manner. FLECs go out of their way to encourage others, becoming devoted friends.

FLECs enjoy studying theoretical subjects that stimulate their imaginations, especially when it relates to people. English, literature, psychology, religion, and communications are all of interest to the FLEC, though they will occasionally venture into the hard sciences, as well.

As Left-brained Conceptuals, highly adept in Wernicke's semantic processing area, FLECs are naturally proficient with abstract understanding of language. Words are their specialty, along with the meanings attached to each. FLECs can become excellent writers. They like to read, as well, especially about people. History is of particular interest, as they are fascinated and inspired to learn about how others lived their lives.

III-3 FLEC Traits

Appearance

- attractive
- tastefully and masterfully (and appropriately) dressed
- innate sense of style
- warm and feeling smile
- usually well groomed, not overweight
- demure, having a feeling and intelligent look
- even-tempered, graceful countenance

Personality

- socially sophisticated
- graceful in demeanor, charming, amiable
- women usually refined
- driven, polite, well-mannered
- leading lady, charming gentleman
- very aware and concerned about appearance
- always looking to help
- carry the hurts of others on own shoulders
- empathetic, considerate
- often a low-key extravert
- capable leader (normally not forceful)

Athletic Characteristics

- coordinate fine and gross-motor movements but mechanically inclined
- high energy, may be jerky (depending on the sport) though perhaps the most fluid of the dominant Left-brained Types
- workhorses, usually fluid when using the left side (e.g. batting left-handed) but more mechanical from the right
- flexible
- good endurance, high pain threshold
- defensive-minded, team builder, personnel mediator
- play by and tactfully enforce the rules

The male FLEC child may appear to be more of an "introverted" Back-brainer, especially when lacking confidence, or if raised in a low-key environment. Though this shy outward persona may disguise the FLEC's true hardwired design, a high energy level of behavior will reveal their true innate circuitry. FLECs love to accomplish tasks and reach goals.

Family problems may negatively impact the attitude of the sensitive FLECs toward themselves, making them hesitant to take risks or be outgoing. An excessive concern for their own appearance may be a key to properly identifying a young FLEC, though this tendency can be reduced as confidence is gained in other areas.

Acting and music are excellent creative outlets for FLEC children. With the ability to be gifted musicians and vocalists, they can often be found going into entertainment. FLECs can also be fine athletes, though they may require assistance in learning to control their naturally pent-up emotions.

Athletic Characteristics

As ECs, strongest in the third region of the motor cortex, FLECs naturally coordinate the fine and gross-motors. As Left-brainers, however, they are more deliberate and "mechanical" in their action than their Right-brained EC counterparts (III-1, III-2). Of all the Left-brained designs, however, the FLEC may be the most fluid, especially when incorporating the left side of the body, which is predominantly controlled by the Right brain.

FLECs often develop a passion for sports, which they tend to personalize. More than perfecting their skills or winning and losing, FLECs enjoy relating to the people involved in the competition. They bring determination and hustle to the game, often energizing teammates with their infectious enthusiasm.

FLEC athletes are blue-collar types, more apt to incorporate power over finesse. Throwing the ball with velocity or hitting it with strength is generally their specialty.

A high-energy workhorse, the FLEC has good endurance and a high pain threshold. This defensive-minded athlete is an excellent team builder and mediator. FLECs play by the rules and use their natural people skills to see that rules are enforced in a tactful way.

Popular Vocations

The FLEC has an inherent Conceptual vision for maximizing the potential in people and situations. Their dominant Empathetic function gives them great regard for those they work with, often treating the workplace as an extended family. A Left-brained inclination for structure, combined with compassion for the wants and needs of others, makes the versatile FLEC a well-liked leader in a variety of roles.

FLECs are extremely trustworthy and tolerant of others. They go about their work with a passion. Tending to personalize their work, they put feeling and care into whatever they do. Integrity is of the utmost importance to the FLEC, which may explain why they are almost always well-liked by co-workers. Naturally leading with their charming persona, FLECs are seldom openly critical, always managing to see the good in others.

Frequently found in areas where they can provide assistance and guidance, FRECs become teachers, coaches, and counselors, while also gravitating toward careers in psychology, ministry, and health-related professions. As teachers, they are frequently recognized as student favorites.

They are also drawn to the business world in advertising and sales. The versatile FLEC may be found in virtually any vocation involving people and ideas, including writing, photography, news media, and interior design. They naturally flourish in any environment where there is constant contact with other people.

Well-Known FLEC Designs

Many well-known FLECs are found starring on the big screen. **Robert Redford** and **Tom Selleck** have personified the suave, alluring FLEC male, while **Elizabeth Taylor** was a legendary leading lady on the silver screen for most of her career.

Other notable FLEC designs in Hollywood include **Julia Roberts**, **Cindy Crawford**, **Brooke Shields**, and **Tom Cruise**.

The world of sports has been impacted by the FLEC, as well. It should not come as a surprise that beloved silver-tongued hall of fame baseball broadcaster **Vin Scully** is a naturally poetic FLEC. Football star turned broadcast legend **Frank Gifford** shared this design, as well. Gifford's natural smooth, low-key delivery served as an ideal complement to the bombastic Howard Cosell during the early years of Monday Night Football.

Finally, perhaps the most adored and "leading lady" of First Ladies, **Jacqueline Kennedy Onassis** was appropriately hardwired for the role she carried out so well.

Performance Keys

The III-3 FLEC is a dominant "feeling" Empathetic. Combined with a strong secondary Conceptual function, this may often result in an idealistic—and unrealistic—view of the world. This can lead to a tendency toward anxiety and emotional letdowns when it comes to dealing with the realities of daily living.

FLECs can combat this by enlisting the counsel of a dominant Sensate, who may be able to help the FLEC more readily work through the realities of the situation. A dominant Analytic may help to provide needed logic, as well, when forced to deal with an emotionally charged decision.

Internally, the FLEC can be mindful to take note of tangible facts, which will provide helpful reference points as events come together. Keeping emotions under control is key for this dominant Empathetic. With a tendency to carry the weight of the world, or at least that of others, keeping the facts of life in mind can provide vital reality checks in order to maintain a healthy balance.

A small percentage of FLEC females may tend toward eating disorders. As Front-brained ECs, they are driven to succeed, often caring tremendously what others think of them. If they become preoccupied with their weight, they may be tempted to employ unwise and unrealistic health habits. It is critical for FLECs to accept themselves as they are.

When FLECs are despondent, they can become physically immobilized. Depression affects them differently than many other designs. For optimal health, it is imperative that FLECs maintain a balanced view of logical reality regarding life's concerns and dilemmas.

III-4 BLEC — "Caring Counselor"
BACK, LEFT-BRAIN (Q4), EMPATHETIC, CONCEPTUAL
(methodically classifies imaginations personally)

Order of Function Dominance: *CONCEPTUAL*, EMPATHETIC, Analytic, sensing

Appearance
The low key III-4 BLEC presents a soft-spoken demeanor with a normally slender build. Wide-eyed, with a conservative, yet feeling smile, the BLEC may have a somewhat unconventional appearance. Modest, conservative attire will generally accompany an orderly, organized look. BLECs will often be found wearing spectacles.

Fewer words, along with a softness in their voice and lower overall energy level can be useful clues in differentiating the III-4 BLEC from the closely related III-3 FLEC.

The four Back-brained Conceptual designs appear to be among the least commonly found in America, and the scarce BLEC may be the rarest of all.

Personality
BLECs are so people-oriented that their Empathetic concern may often provide the appearance of an "extraverted" Front-brainer. As dominant Conceptuals, hardwired in the Left brain, they are constantly giving consideration to ideas their mind generates. These thoughts are generally concerned with helping or improving the lives of others.

As Left-brainers, BLECs are organized and decisive, with a willingness to put in long hours on the job. They will work tirelessly to finish a project as they move toward a clear goal they have formulated.

Though they may be lacking in self-confidence and sensitive to criticism, BLECs tend to see the best in others, relating to those around them with warmth and compassion. They often feel compelled to work for the betterment of humanity. This others-centered disposition is what often gives the Back-brained BLEC the appearance of a high-energy Front-brainer, especially when energized to work toward a cause that will benefit others.

While they do not naturally seek the spotlight, BLECs are

tremendous wordsmiths, often written more than spoken. They love to read, finding the world of books to be a safe haven for their active imaginations.

Children

Young BLECs are daydreamy sorts, with a quiet persona that may present the appearance of complacency. Their mind, however, is far from sedentary. As dominant Conceptuals, they may be idealistic, with a variety of interests. As secondary Empathetics, they are interested in people and history. This EC combination leads to a romantic, sometimes idealistic and impractical mindset. Their vivid imaginations become evident as they relate their visions.

It may not be until the teen years that BLEC children are ready to confidently venture out into the world of reality. BLEC youngsters are sometimes slow to walk and talk, appearing content to watch the world outside, while they remain in quiet contemplation and reflection. When they do finally decide to emerge, BLECs feature a rich imagination, which they frequently incorporate in creative writing.

While the Left-brained BLECs are orderly in their ideas, that organization may not necessarily translate to their physical environment. As dominant Conceptuals, their powerful imaginations may lead them to easily overlook the clutter. This may leave them prone to losing things rather easily at times.

The innate daydreamy nature of this generally well-behaved design can be a problem in school, as well. The BLEC may need to be seated near the front of the class in order to maintain proper attentiveness. BLECs may also be easily distracted by their Empathetic interest in those around them. While they are inclined to do well academically, they may not flourish until reaching the higher levels of education.

Identifying BLEC children is important in order to give them proper time and opportunities to express themselves, especially verbally. Because their motor movements may likewise be slow to develop, early training and patience in that realm is also helpful. This will enable BLECs to better cultivate their coordination and athleticism.

III-4 BLEC Traits

Appearance
- modest, conservatively clothed
- organized
- conservative feeling smile
- often wearing spectacles
- usually slender, wide-eyed, soft-spoken
- unconventional appearance

Personality
- kind
- moderate, shy
- wordsmith
- structured, reticent, reserved, idealistic
- may be unsure of self, sensitive to criticism
- aloof
- interested in people and history
- variety of interests which may require time alone
- may be impractical
- industrious
- organized and decisive
- others centered
- romantic

Athletic Characteristics
- coordinate fine and gross-motor movements, but mechanically inclined
- good hustlers in the game field
- injury prone, soft, yielding
- can be clumsy and awkward
- inflexible, timid
- defensive-minded
- always play by the rules and appreciate the opportunity to play

Athletic Characteristics

As with all region III ECs, the BLEC can develop body harmony, yet will need to work at an early age to combat the inherent **B** and **L** limitations. With a naturally lower Back-brained energy level, and deliberate Left-brained movements, the unrefined BLEC will often display particularly awkward motor skills.

As naturally studious designs, BLECs are deep thinkers, creatively pondering the "big picture" of their sport. They will work long and hard to improve their skills, though the inherent limitations of their hardwired circuitry will inevitably leave them more clumsy and awkward than other designs. They are good hustlers when in the game, giving their all, though normally from a defensive-minded standpoint. Even there, they will have a tendency to be relatively soft and yielding when the proverbial push comes to shove.

Being a regimented Left-brainer with naturally ungainly physical abilities leaves the BLEC especially vulnerable to mishaps on the playing field. As a result, BLECs are generally more injury-prone than most other hardwired designs.

BLECs enjoy playing the game and play it by the rules, accordingly. They value both the inherent structure that rules provide, as well as the nature of fair competition with their fellow athletes.

Popular Vocations

Though often hidden in the work setting, the personable and creative BLEC can be a valued member of any team. Driven to contribute to the welfare of others, BLECs naturally help to foster an atmosphere of harmony and efficiency.

A natural wordsmith, the BLEC expresses superior Conceptual vision with expert writing, which is often favored over the spoken word. As such, BLECs are often drawn to the world of journalism, both writing and editing, along with other media specialties.

BLECs are ideal members of any support staff. Their Q4 hardwiring provides them with innate skills of organization and decisiveness, while their strong Empathetic function leads to easily working well with others. The loyal and sacrificial BLEC can often be found working diligently to make others a success.

In addition to writing, their creative vision can manifest itself in architecture, as well. Virtually any career involving people and ideas can be appealing to the "possibility thinking" BLEC. Psychology, psychiatry, therapy, counseling, ministry, and scientific research are all common vocations for this rather uncommon design. Teaching and social work may also be attractive pursuits.

Well-Known BLEC Designs

Because the low-key BLEC rarely seeks the spotlight, not many are well-known. The few that are have unsurprisingly come from the world of sports. More specifically, an unmistakable height advantage has helped a pair of BLECs to overcome other inherent limitations.

6-foot-11 **Chris Dudley** played 16 years in the NBA, despite being known as a generally clumsy player and one of the worst free throw shooters in history. The likeable Dudley briefly entered politics following his playing career, with encouragement from others and most certainly a desire to serve his fellow man. However, he lost an extremely close election for governor of Oregon in 2010 and just as quickly disappeared from the high-profile political scene.

Another NBA center, **Jim McIlvaine**, was known primarily for his ability to block shots. Though he averaged only 2.7 points per game, the 7-foot-1 McIlvaine lasted seven years before a series of injuries put an end to his NBA career.

Performance Keys

As one of the ultimate "possibility thinkers," the III-4 BLECs have a tendency to take on the world's problems as their own, causing them to often become overwhelmed rather easily. These dominant Conceptuals may become filled with lofty visions of grandeur as they seek to bring harmony among people in every area of life. When these unreachable goals are left unfulfilled, frustration and emotional despondency may ensue.

BLECs must be willing to accept the fact that their romantic ideas may be flawed by the inherent limitations of the real world. They must acknowledge life's imperfections and not get bogged down trying in vain to impose their will on others. They must learn to deal with conflict by facing the unpleasant truths of life.

Enlisting the trusted counsel of an Analytic Sensate can help to provide balance to the BLEC's often utopian imagination.

Rather than discouraging awkward BLECs from participating in athletics at an early age, quite the opposite is true. In order to ensure a commitment and continuation to exercise throughout life, young BLECs should be exposed to and encouraged to participate in athletic pursuits they enjoy. Developing their motor skills early in life will not only help them to better compete, but will provide life-long benefits.

Learning to control anxiety and emotions with mental exercises will prove beneficial. Placing an emphasis on energetic play will also help this naturally energy-conserving design.

12
Region
IV
Analytic Conceptuals

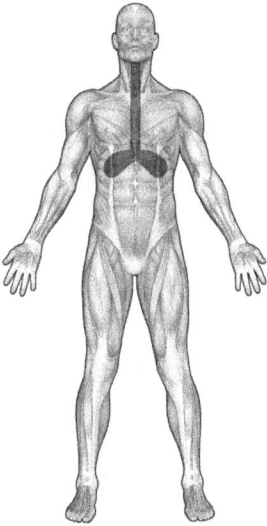

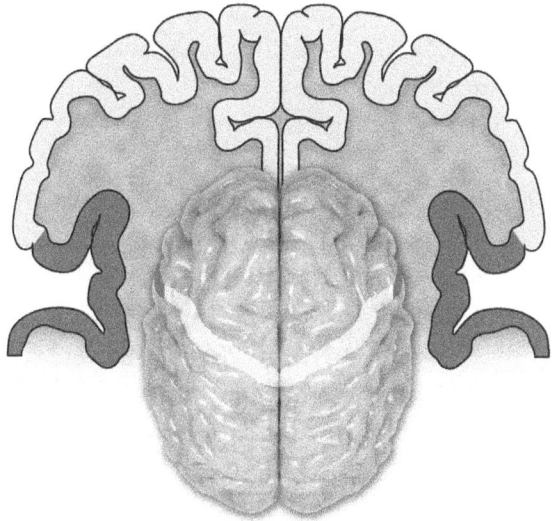

AC **Body Skill Group**

IMAGINE IMPERSONALLY

Region IV - Analytic Conceptuals
Diaphragm Region Skilled

Though not all "Impersonal Imaginers" are wise, most have a high desire to be so—especially in their chosen area of interest. Taking great pride in being competent in whatever they put their fertile mind to, Analytic Conceptuals are very inquisitive, with a continual thirst for knowledge.

ACs come in the widest variety of personas of all groups. They may often become actors, scientists, lawyers, politicians, doctors, college professors, or computer whizzes—but they may just as well be found driving an 18-wheeler, a school bus or a bulldozer. Most ACs are highly industrious and will do whatever it takes to succeed in their chosen profession. They normally enjoy being entrepreneurs in some form.

Often finding their inspirations and revelations in the quiet hours, when daily distractions are gone, ACs have a tendency to "burn the midnight oil" far more than any other designs. ACs prize strategizing and strive for scientific accuracy in their academic or vocational pursuits.

Young ACs usually develop a passion for knowledge very early in life. As children, they are typically very precocious, asking endless questions and longing to get out into the world where they can explore and continue their quest for knowledge. With proper study, it becomes rather easy to spot these AC children, whose exceptionally inquisitive minds set them apart from other kids. They also tend to have particularly good diction.

IV-1 FRAC — "Creative Strategist"

FRONT, RIGHT-BRAIN (Q1), ANALYTIC, CONCEPTUAL
(quickly explores and responds to imaginations impersonally)

Order of Function Dominance: *CONCEPTUAL*, ANALYTIC, Empathetic, sensing

Appearance

The IV-1 FRAC is the most commonly found of all the hardwired designs, especially in the United States. At the same time, this multifaceted design is the most diverse in both appearance and persona, which often leads to confusion with conventional personality inventories. As natural actors (and actresses), FRACs can take on virtually any role to which they set their mind. This makes them often easy to confuse with other hardwired designs, especially to the inexperienced or less discerning eye.

Many FRAC men may have a "computer geek" look. Often living life predominantly in their minds, they may be oblivious not only to current fashion trends, but to their appearance, as well. Both males and females may have a tendency to be overweight and appear relatively disheveled in clothes that don't match. Men frequently display signs of male pattern baldness.

Conversely, FRACs can be flashy if they choose to take on the role of trend-setter with "original" fashionable clothing or by sporting a unique new hair style. They can even appear flamboyantly muscular if naturally gifted in such a way.

The FRAC wants to be competent in whatever they put their mind to, and will have a tendency to let other areas go, accordingly.

Personality

FRACs are energetic, optimistic, and very comedic, often employing a wide range of voice inflection in their speech. Highly verbal and often at a high decibel level, these precocious designs are naturally theatrical, easily exaggerating both content and delivery as they interact with the world. With a witty, quick-thinking mind, they are masters of one-upmanship.

As eccentric non-conformists, FRACs are willing to take risks today as they willingly gamble on the possibility of a better tomorrow. FRACs are creative and goal-driven. These master strategists enjoy tackling challenges and take pride in moving to the beat of a different drummer. Their high-energy Q1 AC circuitry is expertly designed for multi-tasking, though it can also be vulnerable to ADD when it goes awry. This can lead to a very cluttered workplace, as several projects in various stages of completion may sit amongst the undertaking that has captured the FRAC's attention in the moment.

The entrepreneurial FRAC is not only a "jack of all trades," but also a "jack" of all personalities. While the high-energy hardwiring of many FRACs is self-evident, some are more outwardly reserved. They may even claim to be "introverts." Careful scrutiny, however, will reveal the high energy levels of the mind in the true FRAC. Truth be told, they are only "introverted" because they would rather spend time with the most competent person they know—themselves—than to "waste" it with others they deem having little to offer.

Finally, as a go-with-the-flow Conceptual Right-brainer, the FRAC may be characterized by inconsistent and unpredictable behavior. As with all designs—but especially with the highly adaptable FRAC—upbringing and other environmental factors can play a significant role in shaping the persona of these supreme actors.

Children

As precocious children, FRACs often play with their toys in a unique, inventive manner. They may ask a non-stop string of questions throughout the day, with their favorite being, "Why?" Not content to simply play with toys, FRACs want to know how they work. They may take them apart just so they can put them back together. As dominant Conceptuals and strong Analytics, flexible Right-brained FRACs excel in technical mechanics.

With a thirst for knowledge that is often not quenched by the time the sun sets, FRACs are commonly found burning the midnight oil. From studying or reading to another mental exercise, FRACs often have difficulty getting their high-energy Q1 AC mind to calm down enough for sleep. Even as toddlers, FRACs may be found climbing out of the crib in the middle of the night in their quest to explore.

With a non-conforming mindset and armed with an inordinate accumulation of knowledge, young FRACs may not fit the routine structure of standard elementary classrooms. If they fail to find the

IV-1 FRAC Traits

Appearance
- men may have "computer geek" look, often overweight and disheveled, appearing oblivious to fashion trends
- conversely can be flamboyantly muscular if naturally gifted in appearance (usually to one extreme or other)
- attention-getting, flashy
- often take the role of dressing fashionably and trendily
- may relish presenting an "original" hair or clothing venture
- COMEDIC, with wide range of voice inflection

Personality
- energetic, optimistic, witty and swift
- non-conformist, eccentric, dramatic
- willing to gamble on and look ahead to the future
- highly verbal, loud, theatrical, exaggerated, precocious
- actor/actress supreme
- enjoys challenges, prefers juggling many tasks at once (literally and figuratively)
- master of one-upmanship
- may be inconsistent, unpredictable
- very opportunistic, sultan of spontaneity
- chief entrepreneur, often spends more than can afford
- widest personality variety of all hardwired designs (some may even appear reserved)
- jack of all trades

Athletic Characteristics
- more fine-motor than gross-motor fluidity
- bendable, pliable, flexible, not restricted by any particular motor muscle group
- highly energetic, quick thinking
- often utilizes unorthodox methods
- spontaneous, more offensive-minded naturally but also gifted defensively
- may need to become more teachable
- strategic, often breaks the rules of the game and/or creates own set of rules.

teacher or subject matter engaging, they may well disappear into their fertile Conceptual mind for more stimulating thought. As masters of Q1, which specializes in quickly processing new information, FRACs get easily bored with everyday and mundane matters. It should not come as a surprise that a high percentage of children diagnosed with Attention Deficit Hyperactivity Disorder (ADHD) possess the FRAC hardwired circuitry.

Even if they do find the day's topic of interest, the wily and audacious FRAC may seek to challenge the teacher's methods and conclusions with logic and competence. This one-upping expert may also be known to interject a quip at any point in the discussion in hopes of getting a laugh from peers.

Often humorous and entertaining, with an uncanny ability to think on their feet, FRACs possess an unmatched ability to pull off an improvisational stand-up comedy routine. It is no surprise that the vast majority of professional comedians are hardwired with the quick-witted FRAC circuitry.

FRACs are forever curious. Rules may be bent and policies stretched, all in the name of exploring ideas and trying new things. With an ability to expertly improvise, the musically inclined FRACs are expert composers. They have a particular giftedness with music, especially tone, melody, and timbre. They frequently play instruments, doing so quite capably even without the ability to read music.

Though not necessarily blessed with the most natural coordination, FRACs can become excellent athletes, especially if they start young. Master strategists, they seek a creative path to victory with their mind as much as with their body.

Athletic Characteristics

We have now reached region IV of the Primary Motor Cortex—the section furthest from the region I base, which controls the gross motors. The AC designs, which reside here, have the weakest natural gross-motor control. If they do not work to gain coordination in their formative years, many ACs can appear uncoordinated in their athletic movements. The high-energy, loosey-goosey FRAC may appear particularly clumsy if put in an unfamiliar position.

With experience, however, the cunning, resourceful FRAC can

rank among the best athletes in their class. With pliable bodies and quick-thinking minds, these "Creative Strategists" compete with their brain as much as their brawn. Willing to incorporate unorthodox modes of attack, the ingenious FRAC may find a way to exploit even the smallest crack in both the opposition and the rules.

FRACs can generate tremendous whip in their legs and arms—another aspect of being hardwired at the opposite end of the motor cortex from the gross-motor specialists. They often have the hardest serves in tennis and are frequently among the longest kickers in football. Their muscles also may remain looser under pressure than those of the gross and fine-motor dominant Sensates. Many of the top closers in MLB have been FRACs.

The FRAC loves to learn, and may often be self-taught in many ways. Perhaps more than any design, FRACs are willing to experiment with different strategies and methods, even in the midst of a game, just to see if they can come up with a new or improved tactic.

Popular Vocations

As masters of ingenuity and one-upmanship, FRACs enjoy outwitting the system, just to see if they can. As would be expected, they can succeed in virtually any realm to which they put their mind and channel their passionate energies. Visionaries with scientific minds, FRACs approach problem solving with creative logic, offering innovative, imaginative solutions.

FRACs are inspiring, enthusiastic, outspoken, and enjoy arguing either side of an issue, often just for the challenge. They react quickly and resourcefully when placed in a predicament, taking pride in remaining open to new information and possibilities. With the ability to become proficient with so many different things, they may become bored with the same routines, leading them to move on to new jobs or even new careers.

Computer technology, mathematics, science, medicine, strategic planning, and business management are all frequent vocational directions for the entrepreneurial FRAC. They are naturally the number-one defense attorneys, able to skillfully argue virtually any position or cause. They are often artists and musicians, as well, frequently found throughout the entertainment world.

Well-Known FRAC Designs

Will Farrell, **Robin Williams**, **Bill Murray**, and **Eddie Murphy** personify the natural comedic nature of the FRAC, while **Bill Gates** and **Steve Jobs** characterize the high energy in the mind. Renowned entrepreneur **Mark Cuban** represents the not atypical mix of both.

Some of the best servers in tennis have been FRACs. **Pete Sampras**, **Andy Roddick**, **Roger Federer**, and **Pancho Gonzales** all share the FRAC hardwired circuitry, while FRACs **Bruce Sutter**, **Lee Smith**, **Jeff Reardon**, and **Rollie Fingers** rank among MLB's all-time greatest closers.

Inspirational British statesman, **Winston Churchill** was a largely self-taught FRAC, as was prolific composer and performer, **Wolfgang Mozart**, another probable FRAC.

Performance Keys

The high-energy IV-1 FRAC loves life and tackling the challenges that come with it. As their vivid imagination draws them to new projects, situations, and activities, they may leave others left undone. Being accountable to finish what they start will help to ensure that FRACs do not spread themselves too thin.

On the other hand, their innate demand for competence in every undertaking may also lead toward a tendency for procrastination when it comes to tasks or activities they do not feel they perform at a satisfactory level. For tasks they do not enjoy, like cleaning out the garage or tidying up their workspace, it may be helpful to break the job up into smaller chunks that can be more readily tackled in a smaller amount of time. For a more challenging endeavor, such as playing an occasional round of golf, it will help the FRAC to focus on the pleasure of the opportunity to enjoy some outdoor recreation, rather than getting hung up on the inherent frustrations of the game.

FRACs become easily bored with routines, but can accomplish nearly any task if it captures their interest. When projects become boring, however, the FRAC's marginal organizational skills can become apparent and deficient (unless they have been well-trained otherwise). They may need to give extra effort to following up and providing structure to their job-related activities. Enlisting the assistance of an innately organized Left-brainer can be helpful.

IV-2 BRAC — "Einstein"

BACK, RIGHT-BRAIN (Q2), ANALYTIC, CONCEPTUAL
(deeply compares and appraises impersonal imaginations)

Order of Function Dominance: *ANALYTIC*, CONCEPTUAL, Sensing, empathetic

Appearance

The no-frills IV-2 BRAC is one of the least commonly found designs. BRACs are often characterized by a "head-in-the-clouds" look, accompanied by an abstract demeanor. They will normally be dressed in conservative, possibly unconventional attire. When finally moved to speak, the BRAC will tend to do so in a somewhat low-key, monotone voice.

With wide eyes, normally behind a pair of spectacles, the BRAC often characterizes the classic "absent minded" (yet brilliant) professor. They also may be found to have naturally curly hair more frequently than that of most other designs.

With a deep, inward-looking hardwired circuitry, the BRAC may seem oblivious to their surroundings and relatively unconcerned with their outward appearance.

Personality

The highly intelligent BRAC generally has a quiet, approachable demeanor. Patient and scholarly, BRACs choose their words carefully, giving thought to how they wish to share insights from their fertile mind. Even then, they may be difficult to understand, as they relate their thoughts at a higher level with more depth of subject matter than most others to whom they relate. Young BRACs may even eschew speaking altogether at an early age, more concerned with exploring the inward reaches of their mind than relating their thoughts outwardly.

BRACs are supreme problem-solvers, gifted with the ability to organize themselves for effective research. They live in the creative world of concepts and ideas, placing greater value on the principles behind the facts than on the facts themselves. Due to the deep thought and study BRACs give to issues, they often tend to come across as principled, determined, and stubborn, unwilling to compromise their stance.

Though not necessarily anti-social, BRACs are innately drawn more to answering the questions of life rather than engaging in frivolous chatter. They are more apt to be found spending the weekend holed up in the laboratory than to be spotted at a party.

Children

Generally precocious children, BRACs are abstract logicians and often quite reserved. They may be solemn and independent, with a passion for asking "why?"—when they feel like talking—or more often, seeking to determine "why" all by themselves.

Albert Einstein, whose complex and brilliant mind aptly represents this design, spoke little prior to the age of three. His mother was even concerned he had a learning disability, such was young Albert's lack of outward expression. He also showed little interest in befriending other children. Little did his family realize that Albert's amazing brain was already going so deep that it probably considered mere words to be relatively superfluous.

Young BRACs are often not socially adept. They require effort to develop interpersonal skills. They may be chided by others for their tendency to get lost in thought, leading them to increase their personal isolation as a defense mechanism. Until they find more commonality in a college setting, BRACs often feel they are very different from others, though this feeling may be effectively reduced if the BRAC is raised by a Sensing parent or in a more energy-expending Front-brained environment.

BRACs are original thinkers, enjoying logical reasoning for its own sake. With a passion for exploring questions that begin "What would happen if...?," they are highly effective in organizing themselves for research and discovery. As premier problem-solvers, any project, big or small, presents itself as a stimulating challenge.

The precocious mind of the BRAC generally finds little use for the rote learning environment of many classrooms. They typically find the rigorous discipline of lower education to be boring and militaristic. BRACs are unparalleled in problem solving, relying upon their unmatched synthetic and abstract logic of the Right hemisphere.

Because of their extremely competent cerebral abilities, BRACs

IV-2 BRAC Traits

Appearance
- often wearing spectacles
- can dress both conservative or unconventional
- abstract demeanor, "head-in-the-clouds" look
- no fluff
- normally a soft (more monotone) voice
- often has curly hair
- wide-eyed
- absent-minded and brilliant professor
- seemingly unaware of surroundings
- unconcerned with outward show or appearance

Personality
- quiet, approachable
- intelligent, brilliant
- patient practitioner
- select words circumspectly
- studious, bookish, academic, scholarly
- knowledgeable, competent
- principled, determined, stubborn, uncompromising
- may be difficult to understand (relate to)

Athletic Characteristics
- more fine-motor than gross-motor fluidity
- may develop better gross-motor incorporation and fluidity with practice
- strategic, gifted cerebrally
- no dominant muscle control, often awkward, unrestricted movements
- gravitate to solitary over team-oriented athletic pursuits
- defensive, seldom interested in performing in athletics (mostly academic)
- good endurance and pain threshold
- plays by the rules even if no one else will

are most often attracted to academic pursuits. They are frequently valedictorians, especially at the collegiate level. They are far less inclined to pursue athletic activities, unless motivated by parents, siblings, peers, and others.

Athletic Characteristics

BRACs will generally gravitate to academic over athletic endeavors, leaving their motor skills lacking in development. This can leave them with an awkward appearance, lacking gross-motor control and unrestricted, loosey-goosey movements. When they do apply their attention to athletic development, they are capable of developing fine fluidity.

As an AC, hardwired in region IV of the motor cortex with superior command of the diaphragm, BRACs are gifted with potential for breathing mastery. Not surprisingly, many of these thoughtful Back-brainers seek their athletic pursuits in the solitary form of distance running and similar endurance-oriented activities.

The IV-2 BRAC shares Q2 and Analytic similarities with the II-2 BRAS, which is one of the top designs for athletic competition. However, the Conceptual/Sensate contrast results in a world of difference. Though the BRAC does not possess the superb motor skills of the BRAS, the two designs share similar mental intensity and toughness. While BRASs often apply this in sports, BRACs normally use it to attack and dominate the books. If BRACs do decide to devote as much time and energy to athletics as they routinely do their studies, however, they can perform at high levels in some sports.

Not surprisingly, when they do pursue athletics, BRACs employ their cerebral giftedness in strategic competition. Though relatively deliberate in their play and more defensive-minded, they can develop excellent endurance and have a high pain threshold.

Long-distance running is an activity in which the solitary BRAC can naturally excel. Tennis is probably the top professional sport for BRACs, though recent advances in high-tech equipment continue to enhance and favor the power game of Front-brainers.

BRACs value well-thought-out rules and participate, accordingly. They are capable of understanding the rules to a level higher than most of their fellow competitors.

Popular Vocations

BRACs live in the creative world of concepts and ideas, and are drawn to careers that enable them to develop these to the fullest. They relish theorizing and philosophizing about the unknown. BRACs make excellent scientists, philosophers, mathematicians, professors, writers, artists, and computer programmers.

BRACs naturally avoid occupations that involve frequent communication and sales of any kind. They prefer to work behind the scenes, normally alone. The will naturally seek a working environment with few distractions and the freedom to conduct thoughtful research in an area they deem worthwhile.

BRACs often become scientists, inventors, and researchers, due to their innate quest for knowledge and understanding. They have the ability to make sense of complex problems and can be impatient with those less gifted intellectually. In business, BRACs demand flexibility and view boundaries and rules as inhibitors.

Well-Known BRAC Designs

Albert Einstein exemplifies the deep-thinking, cerebral BRAC. He incorporated the outstanding synthetic and Conceptual logic of his Right hemisphere to become one of the top thought leaders and problem solvers in history. As a youngster, however, he was considered far from a budding genius. Young BRACs often abhor the often repetitive learning environment of elementary school, feeling it monotonous and restrictive. Many may not come into their own intellectually until college.

Tennis star **Arthur Ashe** was a rare BRAC who found success in the world of sports, becoming the first black American to be ranked number one. Ashe was known for his thoughtful concern for the welfare of others.

Legendary musician **John Lennon** was similarly known for his deep thinking, engaging in political and peace activism as much as his renowned song writing. Fellow BRAC **Steven Spielberg** is considered one of the most influential film directors and producers of all time.

Performance Keys

For the dominant Analytic "thinking" IV-2 BRAC, their Empathetic "feeling" function is their least naturally developed capacity. This may often lead them to coming across as "impersonal" and unconcerned with the feelings of others.

Being Back-brain dominant, they are even more likely to keep their feelings contained. Making it a point to engage the Front brain when working or associating with others will help to develop and cultivate relationships. As Arthur Ashe demonstrated, even natural intellectual superiority can be used for humanitarian purposes when channeled, accordingly.

In dealing with other people, it is important for BRACs to be cognizant and tolerant of others' natural limitations. This, in fact, is a good lesson for all designs and is a principal benefit of comprehending inborn hardwired circuitry.

IV-3 FLAC — "Charismatic Leader"

FRONT, LEFT-BRAIN (Q3), ANALYTIC, CONCEPTUAL
(critiques, acts on, and communicates impersonal imaginations)

Order of Function Dominance: *ANALYTIC*, CONCEPTUAL, Sensing, empathetic

Appearance

The IV-3 FLAC is born with an innate desire to lead. In fact, they find it quite difficult to *not* lead! Displaying supreme confidence, FLACs are natural presidents and CEOs. They are typically found attractively dressed, featuring the latest style. They may often be spotted wearing no socks when going casual, particularly with loafers.

With a classic, "clean cut" hairstyle, FLAC men are characterized by having "good hair." FLACs are normally brunettes, as they are less inclined than most other designs to dye it blonde (or other colors). That said, they may be more easily moved to employ hair color in an effort to keep away the gray.

FLACs naturally make good eye contact when speaking. They often come across as stern, no-nonsense, take-charge people. Their Left-brain dominance causes them to be organized and decisive in their speech, as well as their actions.

Personality

The commanding FLAC can be imposing and authoritative, taking charge and making decisions with aplomb. Ambitious and competent, the FLAC assumes control with a natural ease. This inclination can leave the FLAC appearing "high and mighty," though they can be very diplomatic when called for.

Motivated to be the best, FLACs operate with a single-mindedness for achieving their goals. They earn high honors, both in school, and later in the workforce. They captivate audiences with articulate, well-informed speech. Intelligent and opinionated, FLACs are skilled at manipulating others to accomplish objectives. They are outstanding debaters, readily able to think on their feet as Analytic Conceptuals, yet without the Right-brained tendency to put their foot in their mouth with an off-the-cuff, knee-jerk response.

They may be hesitant to explore new situations or methods before they have accumulated sufficient information or practiced enough to be—or at least to *appear*—competent in their performance.

These natural "CEOs" have the ability to comprehend complex issues and relate them to the layperson with ease. They can be outstanding communicators, public speakers, pastors, and presidents. They usually memorize their speeches and make excellent eye contact with their audiences. Presidential candidates with this gift normally win the debates and votes.

Rarely wavering from their convictions and objectives, they epitomize the characteristics of the commander in chief. FLACs invariably assume the command awarded them due to their intelligence and competence.

Children

FLAC children generally gain friends and followers, as peers admire their talents, as well as their charismatic persona. Even as children, FLACs naturally lead with confidence and authority.

Even young FLACs are aware of their public image and are usually hesitant to try anything new until reasonably sure they will appear competent. They are often inclined to gather additional information or practice a skill in private rather than risk public humiliation. This tendency may give them the appearance of Back-brained "introverts" at times. Once they have gained the requisite self-confidence, however, their high-energy Front-brained hardwiring will become readily apparent.

FLACs are normally driven to do well in school, having the vision to see the long-range value of a good education. They generally need a mental challenge, however, and a variety of learning methods to remain interested. They may feel more competent than some of their elementary level teachers, leading them to engage in debate at times. As with all designs, the values and discipline they are taught will shape their behavior and persona to some degree.

With the typical voracious AC appetite for knowledge, FLACs work to gain a broad understanding in their areas of interest, though not digging to the depths of Back-brained ACs. With their Left-brained language-based Conceptual function, FLACs have an excellent natural facility for memorizing information and linking concepts verbally. No hardwired design has more potential as an

IV-3 FLAC Traits

Appearance
- attractive, dressed in style
- VERY confident looking
- sometimes stern
- organized
- good eye contact
- often low socks or no socks when casual (particularly among the white male community)
- classic model hairstyle, "clean cut," usually brunette

Personality
- competent, precocious
- ambitious, assuming
- can be "high and mighty," high powered
- commanding, imposing, authoritative
- BORN LEADER
- diplomatic, political
- opinionated, can be manipulative
- goal-driven, motivated, single-minded
- in charge
- distinct, articulate, and intelligent speech

Athletic Characteristics
- mechanical (use of the left side will aid in fluidity)
- more fine-motor than gross-motor control
- energetic
- intelligent and calculating
- very strategic
- mechanically and technically sound movements
- little wasted energy
- controlling/coaching mentality
- critical of others when performing
- both offensive and defensive-minded
- play by and know the rules by heart, also use the rules to own foremost advantage

articulator of logic, which is what makes the FLAC such a supreme debater.

Athletic Characteristics

Among the best Left-brain dominant athletes in most sports, FLACs are able to master fine-motor control, featuring technically sound movements with little wasted energy. Strategic and calculating, they are driven to put in the necessary work to learn and perfect their athletic movements. However, they will always be more deliberate and "mechanical" than their Right-brained counterparts.

High-energy strategists, FLACs are the only Left-brained designs who may be as competent on offense as defense. Their natural controlling/coaching mentality carries over even when playing, making them natural field generals.

On the football field, FLACs naturally prize playing the position of quarterback. With an innate desire to lead and to be in control, no position on the gridiron comes close to being the QB.

FLACs utilize their drive and tenacity in athletics to great advantage. Refusing to concede defeat as long as they are still breathing and able to stand upright, FLACs persevere with their indomitable will until the final whistle.

Popular Vocations

As dominant Analytics combined with a secondary Conceptual function, FLACs are supreme strategists. When coupled with hardwired proficiency in the executive control center of the brain (Q3), we have decisive, high-energy leaders, capable of not only formulating a vision, but maintaining control even in times of crisis.

With natural strength in planning and strategizing, FLACs are skilled at visualizing both short and long-range goals. They are able to visualize not only where their group is going, but also to effectively communicate this sense of direction. They naturally incorporate gentle, yet firm persuasion as they effectively share their vision with others.

In the business world, FLACs can be capable salespeople, but quickly assume management and other leadership roles. Their ability to influence and lead, combined with their knack for strategic intelligence is noticeable and valued. They usually make outstanding executives.

FLACs normally manage their businesses very effectively. Though not ones for small talk, their Front-brained "extraversion" usually prompts them to work with and relate to people. They generally have no problem meeting or getting along with others. They also tend to enjoy working with groups of people while leading them toward a common goal. FLACs can be good organizers and show a high degree of intelligence. Their organizations feel secure under their guidance.

FLACs can excel in virtually any vocation they put their mind to, but they derive their greatest satisfaction from jobs that allow them to utilize their gift of abstract logic while leading and inspiring others. In addition to business management, FLACs can be found in politics, financial planning, banking, law, coaching, ministry, counseling, writing, and public speaking.

Well-Known FLAC Designs

It is no surprise that FLACs excel in the world of politics. In fact, some of our most revered Presidents have shared this innate circuitry. **Ronald Reagan**, **John F. Kennedy**, **Bill Clinton**, and **Dwight Eisenhower** all shared the same FLAC hardwiring. Eisenhower, of course, was a five-star army general prior to being elected President of the United States in a landslide. Interestingly, the upstart victor in the 2016 Presidential election, **Donald Trump**, also shares the FLAC inborn hardwired circuitry.

Jack Kemp was a star quarterback in the AFL before embarking on a successful political career. **Roger Staubach** starred at the Naval Academy and then served as an officer in the Navy before starting his hall-of-fame NFL career. Staubach gained the nickname "Captain Comeback" for his uncanny ability to persevere when all seemed lost and lead the team on late game-winning drives. Sound familiar?

Martin Luther King, Jr., **Vince Lombardi**, and **Bill Belichick** not surprisingly all share the gifted innate leadership hardwiring.

Performance Keys

Similar to the BRAC, the IV-3 FLAC is a dominant Analytic "thinker," which leaves Empathetic "feeling" as their weakest natural function. With sometimes quick tempers, impatience, and critical spirits, FLACs may be tough on themselves, as well as others. They are not naturally adept at relating to people, even though their strong egos may deceive them into thinking they are.

Taking pains to be a good listener will pay dividends for the demanding and focused FLAC. Taking time to understand the wants and needs of others, as well as effectively communicating this understanding, can be beneficial in building and maintaining strong relationships. Especially for those aspiring to a career in politics, giving attention to this natural shortcoming may pay dividends in coming across as a compassionate, sympathetic candidate.

FLACs desire to get tasks completed without delay. They despise inefficiency. Others may resist their style of leadership if it is overbearing, lacking in tact or impersonal. FLACs need to take time to get all the facts, listen to those involved, consider the feelings of others and show appreciation. They will find it beneficial to steer away from arguments and confrontations when possible, and to make an effort to be winsome in their directives.

Taking great pride in being competent in all that they do, the FLAC may disdain change, hesitant to try new things. Not only is change a part of life, but they can take solace with the knowledge that their strong work ethic and strategic mind will expedite any learning curve they may need to navigate.

IV-4 BLAC — "Original Engineer"

BACK, LEFT-BRAIN (Q4), ANALYTIC, CONCEPTUAL
(methodically classifies imaginations impersonally)

Order of Function Dominance: *CONCEPTUAL*, ANALYTIC, Empathetic, sensing

Appearance

One of the more uncommon hardwired designs found in the United States, the IV-4 BLAC is not one to grab the spotlight even when present. They are much more apt to let their work speak for them in the form of research, writing, inventions, and other highly skilled pursuits. BLACs work expertly with language, possessing linguistic capabilities second to none.

Generally of slender build, they tend to wear their hair straight and orderly. They are normally dressed in plain, "economical" attire, shying away from expensive clothes, even if they have the money for them.

Though their speech is relatively astute, they generally deliver their thoughts in a slow and deliberate manner, often in a somewhat monotone voice. Hardwired in the opposite quadrant of their normally high-energy animated Q1 AC counterparts, the general countenance of the BLAC is accordingly stoical in comparison.

Personality

As private and guarded people, BLACs possess almost a secretive persona. They are perhaps the most independent of all hardwired designs. Self-governing and self-sufficient, they are known to live solitary, often reclusive lifestyles.

While they come across as modest, BLACs demand high expectations of themselves. They shy away from the limelight, yet take pride in the competence of their work. Highly intuitive as dominant Conceptuals, they employ Analytic logic to design new and efficient systems, as well as striving to improve and perfect existing ones.

Eccentric and unconventional, the enigmatic BLACs go about their work confident in their abilities, seemingly impervious to the criticism of others. They are inquisitive, probing, and curious, delving deep into their work, which is generally in the scientific or philosophical realm.

BLACs want to improve and correct everything that comes along. They research and redesign continuously. Seeking challenges and disdaining routine, they may ignore the feelings of others, complicating their lives at school and work.

Naturally thrifty and cautious, BLACs are much more apt to save than to spend.

Children

With an active imagination and aggressive independent streak, BLAC children can be challenging for even the most conscientious parents. The BLAC child seems almost like a miniature adult at times, competent in decision-making, or at least confident in it. BLAC **Bill Watterson** illustrated the working mind of this design masterfully in his "Calvin and Hobbes" comic strip. As Calvin continually personifies, BLAC children are driven in pursuit of exploration and experimentation.

Born to be highly competent, BLAC children are decisive and theoretical, though they do not have well-developed common sense at an early age. Though they may not seem to require affection and praise, when given sincerely, these can help balance the Analytic child. BLACs may need to be encouraged to spend time with people, as well as with animals, inventions, books, or simply their own imaginations. Self-confident and self-sufficient, they still need to put time and effort into building solid relationships.

Though more than capable of scoring well at school on formal tests, BLACs may be less motivated to learn by way of the usual, factual, step-by-step methods. They may daydream a lot, but can be high achievers if they put forth the effort. Their most difficult academic years, ironically, come in grade school. If they persevere and study, however, they will often be found at or near the top of the class in college.

BLACs prefer to study alone, generally disdaining group learning sessions. Not only do they prefer their private thoughts, but BLACs disdain incompetent or mundane conversation. Unless the study group consists of the erudite, the BLAC will not likely be found in it. Normally developing good study habits, BLACs work hard to get good grades and appear competent with their peers. The operating

IV-4 BLAC Traits

Appearance
- generally slender
- slow and deliberate speech, often monotone voice
- plain clothing (very economical)
- straight and orderly hair
- often stoic countenance
- intelligent speech

Personality
- private, guarded, secretive
- VERY independent
- conceptually logical, quite intuitive, competent
- penny-wise, saver not spender, thrifty, cautious
- modest, prefer the background but with high expectations for self
- eccentric, unconventional, enigmatic
- may be masters of foreign language
- self-governing, self-sufficient, solitary, often reclusive
- inquisitive, probing, curious
- philosophical, delving deep, scientific
- persevering, seemingly impervious to criticism of others
- relate well to children or the elderly

Athletic Characteristics
- mechanical, more fine-motor than gross-motor control
- no dominant muscle control, weak with gross-motors
- gifted cerebrally, strategic, calculating
- awkward, lumbering, deliberate
- movements with restricted mechanization, uneven
- efficient with little wasted energy
- good endurance and high pain threshold
- defensive-minded
- seemingly wrote the rule book, reinterprets the rules and quick to call out those who break the rules

rule of the BLAC is that work comes before play.

As BLACs advance in school, they may begin to encounter more students and professors of the same hardwired design. This can be comforting to the rare BLAC, who often feels alone in beliefs and insights growing up. Entering graduate school in the technical subjects, BLACs may often feel for the first time that they are in comfortable surroundings. BLACs are life-long learners. It is not unusual to find them taking accredited courses well into adulthood.

Determined and strong-willed by nature, BLAC children may need help relating to other children. Developing athletic skills early in life will enable them to compete athletically with the energy-expending Front, Right brained (Q1) children who far outnumber the rare BLAC.

Athletic Characteristics

As with all region IV designs, the motor skill hardwiring of the BLAC is located farthest down the motor cortex from the gross-motors, leaving them with more fine-motor control. Unlike their AC counterparts, however, their Q4 dominance leaves them especially weak with the gross-motors. Even with training in their formative years, BLACs may remain somewhat clumsy and lumbering with deliberate, robotic movements. Without training, this awkwardness is especially pronounced.

Golf is one of the few professional sports suited to the BLAC. Though lacking the natural motor skills of their Sensing counterparts, BLACs are able to develop a simple, proficient swing. Especially with proper development of the motor skills during their formative years, they can effectively craft a repeatable swing that is unencumbered by counterproductive and superfluous movements.

Strategic and calculating, the cerebrally gifted BLAC enjoys virtually any sport or recreational hobby that challenges the mind. These may include sailing, wind surfing, flying (full-size planes, as well as models), target shooting, and chess, among others.

BLACs also possess good endurance and a high pain threshold. They love challenging the limits of the body, venturing into hiking, biking, and mountain climbing. Several of the conquerors of Mount Everest are believed to have been BLACs.

When it comes to rules of the game, BLACs more often than not know the rule book inside and out. In fact, it may almost seem as if they wrote it. They may even use this knowledge to reinterpret the rules to their advantage, quickly calling out those they deem in violation.

As with most Left-brained designs, the BLAC competes with a defensive mindset.

Popular Vocations

BLACs love challenges and detest routine. They will work long hours researching in an effort to improve and perfect virtually anything they come across. If any process can be put into a system of some sort, the BLAC will strive to figure out a way. Whether it be inventing, researching, writing, or even practicing medicine, the BLAC can be found doing a variety of highly skilled pursuits and doing them well.

BLACs work best when they have a continuous flow of challenging assignments. They enjoy observing a system, tinkering with its mechanisms, and employing their creative talents to "make a better mousetrap." BLACs are born inventors, often holding many patents.

Engineering, computer science, medicine, research, and all of the sciences encompass careers where the BLAC will find the challenging intellectual environment they naturally seek. In business, they can be found in management, consulting, and analysis. They may also be drawn to law, missionary work, and linguistic-oriented fields. BLACs enjoy photography, as well.

BLACs are naturally structured and methodical when going about their business. Sales work is generally avoided whenever possible.

It is not uncommon for BLACs to start their professional career on the lowest level of an organization, sometimes even beginning in unpaid internships. From this subordinate position, the BLACs persevere, working their way to the top. BLACs have a vision for the future that few share, and they are willing to wait and work for promotion, with their eyes set on the executive chair.

In the world of sports, BLACs often make their mark as referees and umpires. They are well designed for the role of official, as they are able to work quietly in the background, withstanding inevitable criticism of the close call, confident in their position. They also enjoy the opportunity to control play that the position provides. When found coaching, you can be sure they will have implemented a well-structured system.

Well-Known BLAC Designs

A pair of well-known NBA coaches are each famous for their successful coaching systems. It is no surprise that **Gregg Popovich** and **Phil Jackson** both share the BLAC hardwiring circuitry. **Tony LaRussa** was known as a fervent master of the rule book during his days as a manager in MLB.

BLACs **Tom Kite** and **Hale Irwin** were recognized as two of the most consistent PGA golfers of their era. **Tom Weiskopf** was widely considered to have one of the most admired swings on tour.

When BLACs make it in baseball, it is generally due to harnessing a strong arm. It took 6-foot-10 **Randy Johnson** years to iron out his awkward BLAC mechanics. Once he gained consistent command of the pitches from his electric left arm, however, the "Big Unit" embarked on a hall-of-fame career.

Performance Keys

The Back-brain dominant Conceptual BLACs are prone to focusing on building their systems, alone with their internal thoughts. This may lead to difficulty in building and maintaining interpersonal relationships. They also may not instinctively compliment others. Showing their appreciation does not usually come naturally.

BLACs may need to practice tactfulness and friendliness. By displaying patience with others, and by allowing themselves to be open to contrasting ideas and styles, BLACs may be able to overcome this instinctive hurdle.

The "penny-wise" nature of the BLAC may also discourage them from sharing the fruits of their labor with others. Making a concerted effort to incorporate generosity into their lifestyles may lead to a more well-rounded and fulfilling life.

13

Hardwired
to
Live

With careful consideration of the remarkable revelations presented in this book, it should be plain to see that the potential benefits of understanding human hardwiring are almost limitless. Not only is it rewarding in regard to understanding and dealing with other people, but also for being your *best you*!

Consider the eternal question, *what is the meaning of life?* I don't claim to have the definitive answer, but if it has anything to do with each of us living our life to its full potential, I will submit that hardwired designs provide a useful blueprint for how we might approach such a quest. I truly believe that we are each born with special gifts—special talents that enable us to live a meaningful life. The revelation of hardwired designs helps to reveal those innate strengths, as well as define our specific inherent weaknesses.

Even as computers and machines make an ever-increasing impact on our lives, we must not lose sight of the fact that it is *people* who shape the world. Even most of those automated mechanisms are inevitably intended for the benefit of people in some form. By understanding not only our own innate circuitry, but also the hardwired designs of others in our life, we can collectively move toward living a more fulfilling life.

Breaking Up the Daily Grind

As we move through the daily grind that life all too often becomes, we may frequently fail to give significant thought to ourselves and others. Often, it is only when something of significance is not handled in a manner in which we would prefer do we make it a point to consider what is going on in the minds of others. Armed with the knowledge of hardwired designs, however, rarely will a day go by that you will not find yourself contemplating the behavior and performance of both yourself and others. You will quickly discover that virtually every aspect of life involving people can be positively impacted with the knowledge of this transformative revelation.

By understanding the inherent strengths and weaknesses of both ourselves and others, we are able to gain an informed understanding of how each person is hardwired to behave and perform. We are then capable of making wise decisions regarding how to handle virtually any area of life involving people.

As I have stated time and again throughout this book, it is important to be mindful that there is no such thing as "good" or "bad" hardwired designs. There are simply *different* hardwired designs, which might make certain people more or less optimally suited for specific tasks and assignments. As you should be able to see by now, someone with a particular inborn design is often best served when complemented by another person hardwired with different inherent strengths. *Together*, complementary designs are able to collaborate to make the best decisions and optimally carry out various tasks.

Even people hardwired in a similar manner can appreciate that they may need to give extra attention to areas in which they may not be strong. For instance, a group of people who are all Analytics can still—and often *must*—make decisions involving people. They may simply need to be more cognizant of the fact that extra careful thought must be given to the *feelings* of those involved.

Briefly consider some of the major areas of life and how the positive impact of understanding hardwired designs may be utilized to live our best life.

Children / Parenting

For parents, this insight will prove invaluable when it comes to children. It will quickly become apparent how each child requires different methods of communication. This includes how each child responds to parents' nurturing and discipline in a specific way, depending upon his or her unique inborn design. When you properly identify and understand the specific hardwired circuitry of each individual child, you will be able to adjust the way you interact with each one, complementing the child's uniqueness with a parenting style specifically optimized for each specific design. In addition, by understanding your own hardwiring as a parent, as well as that of your spouse, you will have better appreciation for how to modify or otherwise handle your natural parenting style to best deal with each individual child.

With proper comprehension of each child's unique circuitry, you can help him or her develop healthy relationships with family and friends in order to live life to its full potential. In addition, it will provide unmatched insight when it comes to learning, as well as extra-curricular activities. In short, it will help every child achieve their full potential in whatever area they choose to apply themselves.

By properly identifying a child's inborn design, one can save needless hours wondering what exactly his or her best natural aptitudes are and what he or she could possibly be enjoying most in life. As a parent, it can even provide the ability to discern traits and tendencies of your child's friends, which may be invaluable in guiding the child to making wise life choices.

Within the family unit, inborn differences can now be respected and even celebrated, as opposed to being a point of contention. Better family harmony and direction can be achieved as relative strengths and weaknesses of each family member are understood and appreciated. As children mature and become exposed to potential areas of interest, you will find that you are better equipped as a parent to guide them with confidence into areas where they can thrive and find fulfillment. This includes academics, music, sports and other activities, often leading to future vocations. You will be able to optimize each child's chances for success in any given pursuit.

Learning / Education

Education is a prime area where hardwiring can make a significant impact, as it provides unmatched enlightenment into each student's innate learning style and motivational keys. It can provide insight to help discover the subjects in which each student will most naturally show an interest and what subjects may present more of a challenge. This knowledge can be used to improve study habits and even to address learning disorders. There is not a realm of modern-day education that cannot be enhanced by hardwiring insight.

As every student's strongest and weakest cognitive abilities are identified via their unique personal circuitry, both teachers and parents will be able to effectively and accurately tailor their teaching methods to best fit the specific learning style of each individual student. In addition, the best study habits for each design can be identified and encouraged for optimal comprehension and retention.

As students and teachers gain an understanding of each other's inborn design, they will have more tolerance and appreciation for the varied interpretation and comprehension of the same subject matter. At the very least, all will become aware of the considerable and quantifiable differences among them—wrought not only by experiences (nurture), but by their respective inborn neural circuitry (nature), as well.

Students will gain the ability to identify optimal subjects for study that will pique their interests while, at the same time, be an optimal fit for their cognitive abilities.

Because this insight accurately identifies the specific regions of the brain where each person is strongest and weakest, it can also aid in dealing with deficiencies that contribute to learning and behavioral disorders. For parents who are searching for medication-free solutions in these areas, identifying and understanding a child's innate circuitry can be a critical and beneficial first step in the process.

As higher education is considered, knowledge of hardwiring can provide unparalleled insight in identifying an optimal major on which to focus in preparing for a future career. In addition, it will help illuminate how to identify and prepare for a career that will provide both personal fulfillment and a suitable level of income.

Relationships / Marriage

Hardwiring provides insight that can be extremely beneficial to developing and maintaining a healthy, loving relationship with your spouse. From budding new relationships to long term accords that have seen their ups and downs, knowledge of our hardwired designs can reveal how best to navigate relationally.

It can provide guidance with how to show affection in just the right way so that it will be most favorably received. Rather than relying simply on how *you* might feel and interpret your actions or sentiment, hardwiring illuminates the manner in which the target of your affection wants—and *needs*—to be cherished. Armed with this insight, any misunderstanding in this critical area can be avoided. Similarly, you will be able to predict the needs of your loved one and be prepared to fulfill them—in advance! You will gain insight to better appreciate, respect and communicate, leading to a more harmonious relationship.

You will be able to anticipate areas of potential conflict and move to smooth them over—*before* an argument ever begins! Even when a conflict does inevitably arise, you will possess a custom designed "user's manual" for quickly addressing the matter and avoiding a problematic escalation. Disagreements can be peacefully resolved in a manner that prevents a buildup of resentment or hard feelings.

In many cases, proper comprehension of hardwired designs may even help to avoid entering into a marriage that would be most certainly destined for failure, based on incompatibility. Other factors would certainly play a role, but the power of possessing this insight in the quest to find lasting love cannot be underestimated.

By having the best understanding of yourself and your spouse, you will be able to ensure maximum compatibility and effectively stack the odds of marriage success in your favor. Without question, there is no equal to hardwiring comprehension in identifying an ideal match for a mutually beneficial life-long relationship and cultivating that relationship properly.

Understanding hardwired designs in the realm of relationships will help to increase understanding, appreciation, communication, respect, and harmony.

Business / Vocations

The knowledge revealed by hardwired designs has far-reaching implications in the workplace. From recruiting and hiring new personnel to developing and motivating existing members of your staff, knowing the inborn nature and behavioral tendencies of individual employees can be invaluable. Best of all, these powerful benefits can be realized without the use of costly, intrusive, time-consuming, and *unreliable* questionnaires. With proper training and careful study, this insight can be incorporated into virtually every realm of business.

Even conflict resolution can be enhanced and expedited. Employees will be better equipped to understand each other and work together more efficiently. We may finally be able to realize and benefit from true diversity in the workplace. The optimally productive and genuinely diversified work environment of the future will not be based on such superficial factors as skin color or gender. It will contain a color-blind and gender-blind strategic cross-section of hardwired designs. This enlightened sense of diverse aptitudes and abilities will provide optimal role performance, in addition to a complementary view of issues and situations.

It will also help to achieve maximum efficiency in personnel decisions. Hiring and internal staffing decisions can be facilitated, as each individual's inherent strengths and weaknesses are objectively quantified. The best candidate can be accurately identified for each position and quality employees can be maintained in their optimal role. Best of all, legal concerns related to invasive right-to-privacy questionnaires can be safely avoided, as recruiters are trained to discern and factor in each candidate's innate hardwiring as a seamless part of the interview process.

Management will be impacted as those with an optimal wiring for leadership can be readily identified. These leaders will also learn how to best connect with and motivate those who are being led.

Even sales can be positively impacted, as needs and desires of customers and clients (both present and prospective) can be positively identified—*in advance*. Salespeople will be able to adjust a sales pitch on the fly, as the salesperson learns how to objectively quantify aspects of the target's hardwiring within seconds of meeting.

Sports / Training

As youth sports become increasingly competitive at ever-younger ages, the trial-and-error method of finding a child's best avenue for athletic involvement is becoming a difficult proposition. Hardwiring, with its unique motor skill association, reveals vital information in regard to where each child has the best potential to succeed. Not only does it provide direction toward the optimal sport(s), but it even provides insights as to what position within that sport the child may be best suited. As a parent, you can encourage your child with confidence that he or she has the best odds of enjoyment and success.

Every person is cerebrally designed to perform best in specific sports or recreational events, often even at specific positions. As hardwiring illuminates, this is due to interrelated mental and physical aspects. Spending a lifetime focused on the wrong sport or practicing in an inefficient way can be wasteful and discouraging. Certainly, no one is precluded from pursuing any sport or activity, but an athlete will perform much better at the sport(s) and position(s) within the sport for which he or she is best mentally and physically inclined.

In scouting for new talent, hardwiring provides evaluators with a deep yet straightforward method of objectively quantifying makeup and future potential. In the training process of the athlete, appropriate attention can be given from the beginning to addressing inherent weaknesses. Training programs can also be specifically tailored for each athlete. Some athletes greatly enjoy the training process, with a natural tendency even to over-train (sometimes at the risk of injury). At the same time, others do not enjoy the seeming monotonous and tedious aspects of training in the least. For them, virtually every part of the training regimen needs to be fun—made into a "game" of some sort in order to hold their interest.

Comprehension of each athlete's internal circuitry can help with proper encouragement while preparing for competition. It can also be beneficial in helping athletes handle pressure of the big moments and big games, as well as dealing with the slumps that inevitably hit.

Finally, the subconscious state of "the zone" is something that athletes often experience when they perform at their absolute best. The ability to enter "the zone" (located in the brain's right hemisphere) can be enhanced by properly understanding hardwired designs.

Optimal Health / Weight Control

Understanding the vulnerabilities and tendencies of each hardwired design can help to identify and overcome habits and addictions of all kinds. Various health-related issues, including anorexia, bulimia, dyslexia, depression, and even attention deficit disorder (ADD) can be better understood with the comprehension of hardwired neural circuitry. Subtle compulsions and phobias can be made sense of, as well.

An area of health that concerns virtually everyone is optimal body weight. By understanding one's hardwiring, eating tendencies can be better recognized and strategies put in place to maintain a healthy, yet pleasurable diet. Exercise and recreation programs specifically suited to each design can also be structured and implemented.

Another major health concern is that of stress. By understanding what situations and circumstances naturally push each design's anxiety level into the red, proactive measures can be taken in advance to minimize many of these potential mental hazards. Optimal hobbies, exercise, and recreation can also be selected in order to maintain motivation and help achieve fitness and relaxation goals.

Knowledge of your special areas of giftedness, as well as your vulnerabilities, will help you to maintain focus on caring for your body and mind in the best way possible. Working to develop good habits can be an especially helpful means of battling inherent vulnerabilities.

Attaining an optimal diet (and body) for each hardwired design is critical. In order to get the brain functioning optimally for its design, it is important that we feed it properly. By understanding your specific inherent tendencies, you can more effectively structure a nutritional and supplemental plan of attack for attaining the body—and brain—of your dreams!

Spirituality

Each person takes a unique spiritual journey through life. An understanding of your inborn design will help to not only validate your questions, but also to determine a custom-tailored approach to go about finding answers. Whatever your definition of God might be, an understanding of the manner in which you are hardwired will help you to grasp how you perceive God via your innate style of informational processing. This insight can help you to gain a better understanding of the Higher Power and, in turn, achieve a deeper spiritual relationship.

For members of the clergy, understanding the hardwired designs of members of your congregation can be invaluable. Not only will you be better able to better connect with each person individually, but you may even gain insight how to best tailor your congregation-wide message.

For Christians, hardwired designs can even provide a better understanding of Scripture and its authors, which can also contribute to a better understanding of God. You may gain a deeper appreciation for and understanding of the Bible as you associate your specific inborn circuitry with the probable hardwired designs of Biblical figures.

If you have any connection to church leadership, such as teaching a Sunday school class or a Bible study, this knowledge can make an already meaningful experience even more so.

Best of all, by understanding your individual design, you may gain a meaningful comprehension of how you were specially created, and thus *your life's purpose.* As you seek your life's purpose, knowledge of how you are innately designed can help you to appreciate even more of your spiritual gifts.

In short, innate hardwiring appreciated through the spiritual lens can literally unlock the door to living your most fulfilling life.

Self-Improvement & Understanding

I asked at the beginning of this book if you have ever wondered why you do the things that you do? Do you wonder where your habits, patterns, and way of life originated? Do you ever ponder whether you could achieve more in life by developing a better understanding of yourself (or anyone that you come in contact with)?

Understanding your specific hardwired design will provide you with concrete answers to these questions, as you learn how you share many mental and physical characteristics of well-known people sharing the same design. Best of all, you can train yourself to be like any role model sharing a similar hardwiring. Try as they may, those of the other fifteen hardwired designs will never be able attain the distinct giftedness of your particular inborn neural circuitry.

Identifying athletes, celebrities, historical figures, and other well-known people you admire with a similar design will provide inspiration and particular direction for how you approach life. Select examples have been provided throughout this book. As you become more experienced with understanding hardwired designs, you will become capable of making more identifications on your own. By studying the hardwiring of others, you can learn and see why people of a similar design may be capable of certain achievements, as well as why they may be prone to certain behaviors, mistakes, or shortcomings. This knowledge can provide direction in helping to shape your habits and way of living, accordingly.

The unique way that your brain is wired from conception leads you to behave in certain ways. Even if you continually try to modify your behavior to fit some idealized (either by yourself or others) mode of operation, your brain's unchanging circuitry will continually predispose you to certain conduct and performance. Though we may never change the way we are hardwired, we can certainly learn to optimally manage our inborn strengths and weaknesses.

Better understanding of inherent strengths and weaknesses provides a more enlightened approach to learning new skills and developing new interests. We can also have better tolerance and appreciation for the mindsets and actions of others, as we strive to understand how their innate design may be influencing them.

Hardwired to LIVE!

You have been introduced to a revolutionary breakthrough in human understanding. Though this revelation involves the complex human mind, it has been presented in the most simplistic manner possible.

As you consider the ramifications of this quantum leap in human understanding, the most important takeaway may be the realization that every single person possesses an innate, "genius-level" ability in their specific area of giftedness. Best of all, this understanding transcends the generic and empty "everyone is special" proclamations made so often in today's world of self-help and motivational programs. This unmatched, state-of-the-art method accurately and substantively identifies the specifics of why and how each person has special, God-given talents and abilities.

Being blessed with a design having certain strengths, however, inherently mandates certain accompanying weaknesses. Even a strength taken too far can become debilitating. Striving to become the most complete person we can be is a worthwhile and noble goal. Understanding our inherent limitations, however, is vitally important.

A person with the build of a horse jockey will experience great frustration in a life spent striving to become an all-star basketball power forward. In a similar way, a football linebacker stands little chance of becoming a world-class ballerina.

Your number one goal should be to become the best YOU that you are capable of being. Live life with confidence in all that you do, as you understand your abilities and deficiencies in any task that you undertake.

Be cognizant of your limitations, but relish your giftedness. You are hardwired for life, and you are hardwired to live! That is, you are hardwired to behave and perform in a certain manner throughout your entire lifetime, but you are also hardwired to live a meaningful life. So, know yourself, appreciate yourself, be yourself, and live your life to the fullest!

Notes

1. Annie Murphy Paul, *The Cult of Personality Testing*, (New York: Free Press, 2004), 107.
2. Ibid., 107.
3. Ibid., 137.
4. Ibid., 109.
5. Ibid., 125.
6. *"Who Am I? Who Are You?"* DVD (Vic Braden Productions)
7. Ibid.
8. Nancy Andreasen, M.D., Ph.D. *Brave New Brain: Conquering Mental Illness in the Era of the Genome.* (New York: Oxford University Press, 2004)
9. *"Who Am I? Who Are You?"* DVD (Vic Braden Productions)
10. Ibid.
11. John Godfrey Saxe, *The Blind Men and the Elephant*, Constitution Society, http://www.constitution.org/col/blind_men.htm.
12. Annie Murphy Paul, *The Cult of Personality Testing*, (New York: Free Press, 2004), 133.
13. Justin Peters, "No Sleep Till Touchdown," *Slate*, September 8, 2006, http://www.slate.com/articles/sports/sports_nut/2006/09/no_sleep_till_touchdown.html (accessed June 2, 2016)

The Hardwired Designs

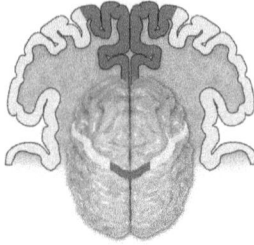

REGION I: EMPATHETIC SENSATE
Observes *Personally*
(Gross-Motor)

I-1	FR**ES**	"Social Performer"
I-2	BR**ES**	"Harmonious Free Spirit"
I-3	FL**ES**	"Personable Provider"
I-4	BL**ES**	"Guardian"

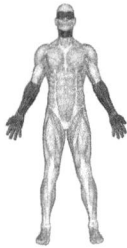

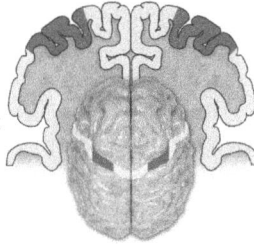

REGION II: ANALYTIC SENSATE
Observes IMPERSONALLY
(Fine-Motor)

II-1	FR**AS**	"Quarterback"
II-2	BR**AS**	"Intense Artisan"
II-3	FL**AS**	"Director"
II-4	BL**AS**	"Perfectionist Inspector"

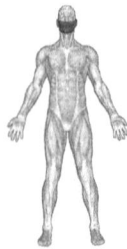

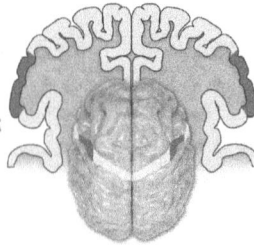

REGION III: EMPATHETIC CONCEPTUAL
Imagines **Personally**
(Mouth region)

III-1	FR**EC**	"Motivational Dynamo"
III-2	BR**EC**	"Imaginative Romantic"
III-3	FL**EC**	"Enthusiastic Teacher"
III-4	BL**EC**	"Caring Counselor"

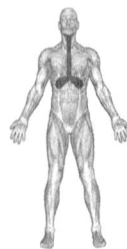

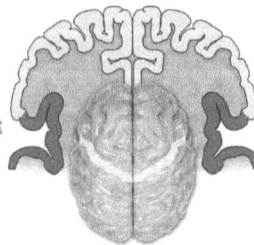

REGION IV: ANALYTIC CONCEPTUAL
Imagines IMPERSONALLY
(Diaphragm region)

IV-1	FR**AC**	"Creative Strategist"
IV-2	BR**AC**	"Einstein"
IV-3	FL**AC**	"Charismatic Leader"
IV-4	BL**AC**	"Original Engineer"

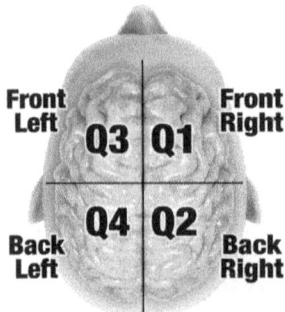

Four Quadrants

Q1 Explore - via what is (**S**) or what could be (**C**)

Q2 Compare - via **E** or **A**

Q3 Critique - Contrast via **E** or **A**

Q4 Classify - Categorize via **S** or **C**

Front Left — Q3
Front Right — Q1
Back Left — Q4
Back Right — Q2